AMERICAN COUNCIL ON EDUCATION STUDIES

FOUNDATIONS FOR TEACHER EDUCATION IN AUDIO-VISUAL INSTRUCTION

By
ELIZABETH GOUDY NOEL
AND J. PAUL LEONARD

SERIES II—MOTION PICTURES IN EDUCATION—NUMBER 9
Washington, D.C.   Volume XI, June 1947

American Council on Education Studies

SERIES II. MOTION PICTURES IN EDUCATION

FOUNDATIONS FOR TEACHER EDUCATION IN AUDIO-VISUAL INSTRUCTION is intended to serve as a practical guide for administrators and teachers of audio-visual education in both public schools and colleges. It suggests the content necessary to the development of both pre-service and in-service programs. It includes the report of the Committee on Developing Standards of Teacher Competency in Audio-Visual Education, California State Department of Education, Division of Audio-Visual Education.

The American Council on Education

EXECUTIVE COMMITTEE, 1947–48

Leonard Carmichael, *Chairman*

Russell M. Grumman	William P. Tolley
Henry H. Hill	Herman B. Wells
Edward B. Rooney, S.J.	Helen C. White
John W. Studebaker, *ex officio*	George F. Zook, *ex officio*

Eugene B. Elliott, *Secretary*

EXECUTIVE OFFICERS

George F. Zook, President
A. J. Brumbaugh, Vice President
Francis J. Brown, Staff Associate
Robert D. Quick, Manager of Publications
Helen C. Hurley, Assistant to the President
Grace R. Ontrich, Chief Accountant
Mary Irwin, Editor

Copyright 1947, AMERICAN COUNCIL ON EDUCATION, 744 Jackson Place, Washington 6, D.C.

FOREWORD

In every developing aspect of education that I have followed over the years, sooner or later the problem of teacher preparation has arisen. New method, new content, or new materials of instruction, whatever is being added to the total educational picture carries with it a concomitant change in teacher preparation. This need for expanded or revised preparation for teaching likewise always has two distinct aspects: preprofessional education and in-service education. The field of audio-visual education is no different in this respect than any of the other newer aspects of education.

Foundations for Teacher Education in Audio-Visual Instruction has been prepared in the hope that it may provide a brief, practical, and easily usable manual and guide for those who are initiating, developing, or revising programs designed to prepare teachers competent in the use of audio-visual materials.

It is my feeling that improved teacher education in the use of audio-visual materials is of the utmost immediate importance, first, because adequate education of teachers in the use of these materials has lagged far behind the development of the materials themselves, and, second, because these materials are applicable over a wide range of subject-matter areas and age levels. It is my sincere hope that this study will assist materially in providing our schools with teaching personnel skillful in the use of these valuable materials of instruction.

George F. Zook
President

April 1947

INTRODUCTION

Foundations for Teacher Education in Audio-Visual Instruction has been prepared to serve as a guide for administrators and instructors in colleges and universities planning to include work in audio-visual education in their pre-service and in-service teacher education program, and for administrators, supervisors, and directors of audio-visual departments in local school systems in planning in-service education programs.

Need for teacher education in audio-visual education has been recognized by many individuals and groups. Official recognition, such as that found in the adoption of the certification regulation[1] by the California State Board of Education, January 4, 1946, can be expected increasingly.

It was a fortunate coincidence that, while the authors were working on preliminary drafts of this study, a Committee on Developing Standards of Teacher Competency in Audio-Visual Education was named by Roy E. Simpson, State Superintendent of Public Instruction in California to implement the certification regulation mentioned above. Twenty-five educators (including the authors), from colleges, universities, and selected school systems were named to this committee which was headed by the chief of the Division of Audio-Visual Education. The committee members were Reginald Bell, associate professor of education, Stanford University; John S. Carroll, county superintendent of schools, San Diego County; N. Evelyn Davis, supervisor of audio-visual education, Long Beach Public Schools; Mrs. Clara St. Pierre Fike, supervisor of audio-visual education, South Pasadena Public Schools; Bruce Findley, assistant superintendent, Los Angeles Public Schools; Frank N. Freeman, dean, School of Education, University of California, Berkeley; Frank F. Gorow, director of audio-visual education, Fresno County; Donald Harrison, deputy superintendent, Stockton Public Schools; Helen Heffernan, chief,

---

[1] "Institutions to be considered for approval to offer the training and to make the recommendation for the kindergarten-primary, general elementary, junior high school, general secondary and junior college credentials must, effective July 1, 1947, maintain a course, or the equivalent, of at least two semester-units in value in audio-visual-radio education and require that such course be successfully completed by each applicant for one or another of the credentials listed above." (California Administrative Code, Title 5, Section 818 (a).)

Division of Elementary Education, California State Department of Education; Walter R. Hepner, president, San Diego State College; Edwin A. Lee, dean, School of Education, University of California, Los Angeles (represented by Malcolm McLean, professor of education, University of California, Los Angeles); J. Paul Leonard, president, San Francisco State College; Frank B. Lindsay, assistant superintendent of public instruction and chief, Division of Secondary Education, California State Department of Education; Dixon Mac-Quiddy, instructional materials co-ordinator, Santa Barbara Public Schools; Carl B. Manner, director of audio-visual education, Vallejo Public Schools; James McPherson, Extension Division, University of California, Los Angeles; Mrs. Elizabeth G. Noel, president, Audio-Visual Education Association of California, Southern Section; Reuben R. Palm, director of secondary education, Los Angeles County; Raymond C. Perry, associate professor of education, University of Southern California; Mrs. Helen Rachford, director of audio-visual education, Los Angeles County; John W. Taylor, county superintendent of schools, Mendocino County; Vernon O. Tolle, director, School of Education, University of Redlands; Ralph D. Wadsworth, principal, University Senior High School, Los Angeles; Curtis E. Warren, city superintendent of schools, San Francisco; and Francis W. Noel, chief, Division of Audio-Visual Education, California State Department of Education, and chairman of committee.

The committee was directed to prepare a report which would serve as a guide to the pre-service education of teachers in this field. In studying the problem of teacher competency in audio-visual education, members of the committee (1) drew heavily on their own experiences; (2) considered the written responses of selected colleges and universities outside of California concerning the content of their audio-visual education courses; (3) studied the results of a questionnaire circulated by the Audio-Visual Committee of the California School Supervisors Association, and (4) examined the preliminary draft of the present study. The committee's report discusses the meaning of the term "audio-visual education" and specifies the knowledges, skills, and abilities teachers need to use audio-visual materials effectively in the classroom, thus providing an accepted and logical basis for suggestions of content to be included in pre-service and in-service teacher education in this area. The final report of the committee is embodied in this publication (see particularly chapters i and iv).

Through the coincidence of the two projects the authors were able to explore opinion, receive assistance, and test their conclusions in a manner which would otherwise have been impossible.

Foundations for Teacher Education in Audio-Visual Instruction does not attempt to outline units of study for a course in audio-visual education. It does, however, present suggestions which can be organized and expanded into units and courses of study and suggests ways teacher education institutions can incorporate these suggestions into pre-service and in-service programs. The objectives are: (1) to clarify the meaning of audio-visual education; (2) to outline the knowledge, skills, and abilities that teachers need to use audio-visual materials effectively in the classroom; (3) to suggest content which should be included in the study of audio-visual education if competency is to be obtained; (4) to indicate means of incorporating this content into pre-service and in-service teacher education programs at the college and university level; and (5) to suggest criteria by which an institution can evaluate its own offerings in audio-visual education.

Chapters i and ii outlining the knowledges, skills, and abilities needed for teacher competence in audio-visual instruction and the content which should be taught if such competence is to be attained may be used as a syllabus by students who are taking courses in this field and by teachers who are participating in workshops or institutes. The references beginning on page 48, which develop sections of chapter ii, will be useful to both students and instructors.

ELIZABETH GOUDY NOEL
J. PAUL LEONARD

April 15, 1947

CONTENTS

	PAGE
FOREWORD	iii
INTRODUCTION	iv
I. THE MEANING OF AUDIO-VISUAL EDUCATION	1
Knowledges, Skills, and Abilities Needed for Competence in Use of Audio-Visual Materials	2
II. SUGGESTED CONTENT FOR MEETING TEACHING REQUIREMENTS	4
Philosophical and Psychological Factors Which Affect the Use of These Materials in the Classroom	5
Research Studies and Their Implications for Instruction	6
Characteristics of the Common Types of Audio-Visual Materials	9
Materials Available in Specific Areas	12
Sources of Materials and Equipment—Local, National, and International	18
Principles of Good Teaching That Affect the Selection and Use of These Materials	25
Production of Simpler Aids, Such as Mounted Prints, Handmade Slides, Filmstrips, and Photographs	32
Principles and Procedures for Setting Up an Audio-Visual Education Service; How a Teacher Can Best Use This Service	34
Current Trends and Practices	38
III. SUGGESTIONS FOR PRE-SERVICE AND IN-SERVICE EDUCATION OF TEACHERS	41
Pre-Service Education of Teachers	41
In-Service Education of Teachers	43
IV. GUIDES FOR THE EVALUATION OF TEACHER EDUCATION PROGRAMS IN AUDIO-VISUAL EDUCATION	45
BIBLIOGRAPHY	48

I. THE MEANING OF AUDIO-VISUAL EDUCATION[1]

AUDIO-VISUAL education refers to the carefully planned and integrated use of a wide range of teaching materials from the kindergarten through the college. Audio-visual education includes the use of field trips or excursions, sound and silent motion pictures, television, objects, models, specimens, dioramas, slides, filmstrips, stereographs, study prints, posters, microphotographs, radio programs, recordings, maps, charts, graphs, and synthetic training devices. It also includes the use of the blackboard, the bulletin board, the hall display case, and similar facilities available in most schools. Instruction is improved by the use of these materials and by life experiences which supplement and clarify the printed word.

Modern educational objectives require improvement in instructional materials and practices, and the dynamic nature of these materials themselves—their content, organization, and manner of presentation—assure that, when wisely used, they will clarify concepts and make learning more meaningful and efficient. Because they can realistically portray things and events in their various relationships, audio-visual materials become an important means of presenting the patterns of modern life rooted in scientific discoveries and technological processes. Because radio, motion pictures, filmstrips, transcriptions, and other audio-visual materials can bring the world, past and present, vividly and concretely into the classroom, they are a means of insuring education against isolation from life. These materials also serve as mediums of modern communication to present current problems and issues. Through the use of audio-visual materials in the classroom for this purpose, learners can improve their study of these problems and their competency in solving them, thus increasing their experiences in citizenship and developing the understandings and attitudes necessary for democratic living.

Audio-visual education, then, is a modern way of teaching and is in harmony with modern educational thinking. Audio-visual education

[1] This first section of the present study is quoted from the "Report of Committee on Developing Standards of Teacher Competency in Audio-Visual Education, California State Department of Education, Division of Audio-Visual Education, December 9, 1946."

is *not* an end in itself; audio-visual materials are tools. In themselves, they cannot adequately meet modern educational objectives. How they are selected and used by the teacher will in a large measure determine the extent to which instruction will be improved.

Knowledges, Skills, and Abilities Needed for Competence in Use of Audio-Visual Materials[2]

The teacher is and must always be the most essential element in the education of children and youth. The utilization of audio-visual education materials calls for more, rather than less, preparation and participation by the teacher.

To realize the values inherent in the tools of audio-visual instruction, the teacher must have certain knowledges, understandings, skills, and abilities. The list presented here is not an outline for a course of study, but rather a statement of basic requirements for teacher competency in this field.

Knowledges and Understandings

1. Philosophical and psychological factors underlying the use of audio-visual materials and equipment in the classroom.

2. Results of research studies, past and present, in the field and their implications for instruction.

3. Physical characteristics and nature of the common types of audio-visual materials and equipment, and the educational values and limitations of each.

4. Types of audio-visual materials available in the specific area of the teacher's interest and their potential educational worth and uses.

5. Sources of materials and equipment—local, national, and international.

6. Principles of good teaching that affect the selection and use of these materials.

7. Processes involved in the production of some of the simpler materials, such as mounted prints, handmade slides, filmstrips, and photographs.

8. Methods of procuring, storing, filing, and maintaining the various kinds of materials and equipment.

[2] The balance of this chapter has been adapted by the authors from the "Report of the Committee on Developing Standards of Teacher Competency in Audio-Visual Education."

9. Principles and procedures for setting up an audio-visual education service in a single school or in a school district; how a teacher can use that service; and the teacher's responsibility for cooperating with the department.

10. Background and development of audio-visual education that have a relation to current trends and practices in the field.

Skills and Abilities

1. Appraising the educational worth, technical quality, photographic characteristics, and commercial aspects of audio-visual materials.

2. Selecting audio-visual materials to meet pupils' needs and the purposes of instruction.

3. Using audio-visual tools effectively in a classroom situation.

4. Evaluating the effectiveness of the use of these materials in teaching situations; modifying and improving future instructional practices on the basis of such evaluation.

5. Assembling and operating various kinds of equipment and performing simple servicing operations such as lubrication and the replacement of lamps.

6. Providing and arranging the best physical conditions possible for using these materials.

7. Planning and successfully executing a field trip or excursion.

8. Producing simple materials, such as mounted prints, slides, posters, charts, graphs, models, collections of natural science materials, and preparing exhibits and displays.

9. Displaying materials effectively on the bulletin board, in the classroom, and in other appropriate locations.

II. SUGGESTED CONTENT FOR MEETING TEACHING REQUIREMENTS

THIS CHAPTER suggests the nature of the content which should be studied if teachers are to gain competence in the use of audio-visual materials. The knowledge and understandings given in the preceding section have been developed only enough to suggest the nature of the content that should be taught and the viewpoints that should be established. No attempt has been made to present a complete discussion of a point, or to outline the activities and experiences needed to assure the development of skills and abilities. However, the bibliography for the present chapter (pages 48–59) will supply further information pertinent to the topics under consideration and will, in some instances, suggest problems and activities for study and practice.

The authors recognize that an academic and merely verbal presentation of facts about audio-visual education will not in itself develop the skills and abilities necessary for competence but that they must be acquired through activities and experiences with the materials and equipment in actual learning situations. These activities and experiences must grow out of the needs of the teachers in a particular group or class and be an integral part of any functional study of audio-visual education. Nothing less will achieve teacher competence in this field.

A teacher who has thus gained a working knowledge of the materials and methods of audio-visual education will recognize that there is no "one best way" to use audio-visual materials and that new methods of use are continually being developed. He will be aware that more and better materials are needed and will feel a responsibility for making constructive suggestions to producers. He will be alert to find or create audio-visual materials which will contribute directly to his classroom needs. He will appreciate fully that the time and effort required to select and use audio-visual materials effectively will be repaid in terms of more and better learning. The teacher will not regard audio-visual materials as a mere supplement to textbooks or look upon them solely as "enrichment." He will, on the other hand, know that under certain conditions the textbook may supplement the film, the transcription, or other instructional tool. Such a teacher will be aware of the fact that many students cannot learn as easily from the printed word as by other means, and will be able to provide suitable audio-visual materials from which students can learn. He will know, too, that the production and use of certain audio-visual materials by the students often constitute in themselves valuable learning experiences. These concepts, and others equally important, will be most effectively developed in an instructional program that avoids the strictly academic and verbal approach and that is itself an example of practical, modern teaching with audio-visual materials.

Philosophical and Psychological Factors Which Affect the Use of These Materials in the Classroom

It is assumed that teachers in service and teachers in training will have had courses in educational philosophy and psychology prior to a general consideration of educational methods and the more specific study of audio-visual education.

If a teacher is expected to make intensive and effective use of audio-visual materials in the classroom, (*a*) he should understand that his relationships with his pupils, the materials he selects, and the classroom procedures he employs reflect his philosophy of education and his understanding of psychology; and (*b*) he should know that the reasons for selecting and using audio-visual materials for instructional purposes are consistent with modern educational philosophy and psychology.

If a teacher conceives of learning as experiencing, then he will try to provide in the classroom those situations and experiences which are personally and socially vital to his pupils. He will be essentially concerned about the development of understandings and attitudes which will affect his pupils' behavior. Likewise, if he believes that there is no reason to separate the mental, physical, and emotional aspects of a learning experience, he will see that what he teaches is affecting the total personality of the pupil. The materials he chooses and the methods he uses will be affected by this premise.

Modern educational psychology emphasizes individual differences among pupils. The students differ in experiences, interests, emotional responses, needs, capacities, and rates of learning. It is, therefore, important that teachers select and use materials which will meet those differences adequately. The many types of audio-visual materials, ranging from the simple print to the complicated graph and motion picture, can help meet the varying needs of pupils. The nature of the aids themselves also makes it possible to treat a single subject in diverse ways: in the study of airplanes, for example, a radio broadcast, a filmstrip, a motion picture, or a model will each contribute something different to such a study and help meet the many-sided interests and abilities of the pupils. And, for many students, the visual presentation of concepts makes them more understandable than the use of words. An understanding of the nature of perception should also result in the teacher using a variety of teaching materials and approaches to the same learning.

Educational psychology also points out that readiness to learn is partially achieved by giving pupils concrete experiences. Audio-visual materials can help provide types of experiences that are more concrete than the printed word; for example, the school journey, models, exhibits, and the motion picture.

Modern educational philosophy, when translated into objectives, points to the need to develop understandings and build attitudes. Psychologists maintain that attitudes direct and motivate behavior and that the emotions are the most important and frequent factor in building or changing attitudes. Teachers should use instructional materials which provide wholesome emotional experiences and which will develop those personal and social attitudes essential for life in a democracy. Many motion pictures, radio dramas, plays, sound filmstrips, if wisely selected and used, can develop attitudes by their dramatic nature and their capacity to present human and social values and relationships.

Other points pertinent to this discussion should be brought out in the consideration of the background of audio-visual education, the research in the field, the nature of the aids themselves, and the principles of good teaching that affect the selection and use of these materials.

Research Studies and Their Implications for Instruction

Some research has been reported in the field of audio-visual education. Briefly, it attempts (1) to make it clear to teachers and those preparing to teach that the educational value of these materials has been well established; (2) to give teachers a knowledge of the types of learning activities which have resulted particularly from the use of motion pictures and radio programs; (3) to show that many of the principles of good classroom utilization stem from these studies; and (4) to make teachers and students who are preparing to teach aware of the problems and areas in which research is needed.

The research which has been done might be discussed and summarized as follows:

1. Research studies to indicate subject-matter areas in which motion pictures have been used effectively. For example, studies by Freeman, Rulon, Arnspiger, and others, have tested and established the value of films in general science, music, history, biology, safety education, and other subjects.

2. Research studies to establish the educational effectiveness of motion pictures in classroom instruction. These include the studies of Rulon, Knowlton and Tilton, Wood and Freeman which provide evidence of the progress students have made in certain controlled experiments. They also include the studies which point to the effectiveness of motion pictures in the learning of facts, in producing the ability to think and reason, and in developing attitudes and appreciations.

3. Research studies to evaluate motion pictures in general education and the methods of utilization in the classroom. The studies of the Motion Picture Project of the American Council on Education are significant here and have implications for methods of selection and utilization at various grade levels and for different educational purposes.

4. Research studies, such as the Payne Fund studies, to establish the social influences of the theatrical motion picture. These studies are significant to education because they establish the fact that motion pictures are effective in developing ideas, attitudes, and emotions.

5. Research to establish the extent to which films and other visual materials were used in industrial and armed forces training during World War II, the ways they were used, and their implications for education. For example, when three hundred individuals who for the most part had served as instructors, supervisors, or psychologists in the armed forces were questioned about characteristics observed in armed services training programs, "more and better use of visual

aids" was the feature receiving the most commendation. On the side of industry, when 239 companies representing a wide variety of industries were surveyed, 62 percent indicated that they used visual aids in their training programs, 75 percent of these used visual aids in more than one type of training, and 84 percent of these planned to continue or increase their use after the war. Hoban, Noel, Vander Meer, and others draw some important conclusions about the wartime uses of these materials and their implications for peacetime education.

6. Research studies to appraise the educational value of various types of radio broadcasts and to evaluate various methods of use. The Evaluation of School Broadcasts Studies conducted by the Ohio State University in cooperation with the General Education Board and the Federal Radio Education Committee are among the more important studies which show that educational changes can result from radio listening. These cooperative studies contain some generalizations about the content and production of broadcasts for schools. Descriptive studies, based on teacher judgments, made by the Evaluation of School Broadcasts Project and the Wisconsin Research Project in School Broadcasting reported ways in which radio broadcasts had demonstrably contributed to the objectives of education. Lazarsfeld's social research in this field also has implication for the place of radio in the classroom as an instructional tool.

7. Research studies to establish the educational values of other audio-visual aids such as the school excursion and the museum. For example, Grinstead's experiment indicated that the excursion technique is superior to class discussion for the teaching of material requiring comparisons and knowledge of concrete objects.[1] Atyeo's study, *The Excursion as a Teaching Technique,* revealed, among other things, that the excursion technique is applicable in all departmental fields and in schools of all sizes. Studies on the best way to conduct visits to the museum show, for instance, that preparation for the visit is most effective when it occurs only one day before the visit and that formal introductory lectures are not necessary for pupils above the fifth grade. Findings such as the foregoing have many implications for altering instructional procedures.

[1] See H. C. Atyeo, *The Excursion as a Teaching Technique* (New York: Bureau of Publications, Teachers College, Columbia University, 1939), p. 172. Here is quoted an excerpt about this experiment from a Master's thesis, University of Southern California, June 1929.

Characteristics of the Common Types of Audio-Visual Materials

By actually handling and using the materials and equipment, teachers will learn the distinguishing characteristics and the nature of the common types which include:

Blackboards
Bulletin boards
Exhibits
Field trips or excursions
Filmstrips (silent and sound), projectors, and screens
Graphic materials (graphs, charts, and diagrams)
Microprojectors
Models
Motion pictures, projectors, and screens
Opaque projectors with specimen and flat pictures
Radios
Record and transcription players
Recorders
Slides, 3¼ x 4, projectors, and screens
Slides, 2 x 2, projectors, and screens
Study prints or flat pictures
Tachistoscopes
Three-dimension materials and equipment

MOTION PICTURES

Motion pictures will be discussed here to illustrate the kinds of information and understandings a teacher should have about this one type. Similarly, knowledge about each aid should be gained from actual experience in handling and using it.

1. A knowledge of the physical characteristics of motion picture films should include the following:

   a) Comparative sizes of 8-mm., 16-mm., and 35-mm. film
   b) Differences between silent and sound film
   c) Difference between positive and negative film
   d) Comparison of color and black-and-white film
   e) Purpose and care of emulsion on film
   f) Reel sizes and weights
   g) Differences between acetate and nitrate bases
   h) Effects of temperature and humidity on film

2. The nature of the medium makes it possible for the motion picture:
   a) To show motion.
   b) To photograph rapid action which appears slowed down when shown at normal speed; for instance, the flight of birds or the movement of insects.
   c) To speed up action. Through time-lapse photography, the film can show action and processes too slow for normal vision, for instance, the blossoming of a flower or the metamorphosis of a tadpole to a frog.
   d) To magnify small objects. Through microphotography, organisms too small for the human eye to see can be photographed; for example, bacteria in action.
   e) To explain theories, to illustrate principles, and to show processes not visible to the human eye. Through animated diagrams, figures, charts, and objects, films can explain, for example, the theory of flight, a geometric principle, or the action of the heart.
   f) To reproduce or re-enact real-life happenings with the elements of drama and emotions inherent in life activities. For example, a film can reproduce the life of the people of India as it exists today, or it can re-enact the life of New Orleans a century and a half ago.
   g) To present continuity of action and show the relationships of people to people, of people to places and things, and of things to things. For example, a film on Mexico[2] shows how the Mexicans live on the land and by the land. This basic theme gives continuity to the entire film.
3. Educational values which are derived from their use:

   The capacity of the film to present subject matter in a variety of ways has just been discussed and such presentations of subject matter in themselves have potential educational values. However, researchers and teachers who have used films in their classrooms assign them other values which depend largely upon the organization and presentation of subject matter, the quality of production, and the way the films are used for instructional purposes. These values are not exclusive to the motion picture and may also be attributed to other visual or auditory materials. Some of the values are given here. References which discuss them more fully appear in the Bibliography (pp. 50–51).

[2] *Land of Mexico*, Encyclopaedia Britannica Films.

a) Motion pictures arouse sustained interest which leads to retention and further investigation through reading and discussion.
b) Motion pictures are useful in the development of attitudes.
c) Motion pictures increase oral responses as well as pupil participation in activities.
d) Motion pictures stimulate the imagination and often lead the student to think critically about a problem.
e) Motion pictures contribute to the learning of factual information.
f) Motion pictures can help develop skills and habits.
g) Motion pictures give an understanding of time relationships, social relationships, and physical relationships.
h) Motion pictures by their capacity to depict action, which is an integral part of life, can present concrete experiences essential for conveying a sense of life and reality.

4. Limitations which teachers should consider:

Many of the unsolved problems in the production and use of educational films are often described as "limitations" of the motion picture itself; however, they tend to disappear as films improve in quality and teachers gain skill in using them. For instance, a frequently mentioned limitation is that motion pictures move at a controlled, uninterrupted tempo, often too fast for students. This is primarily a criticism of particular films rather than a basic limitation of the medium. The fact that a sound film runs through a projector at the uniform speed of twenty-four frames a second does not mean that the action within a given scene must likewise be rapid and unchanged. Action can be slow and sustained, scenes can be long or short, speech can be measured, normal, or fast. All of these factors are dependent upon the direction and editing, and, in so far as instructional films are concerned, upon the producer's understanding of certain educational principles, the psychology of learning, and the findings of research in the field.

Other limitations not intrinsic to the film itself include such criticisms as "the film is too long," "the vocabulary is too difficult," and "it covers too much territory." None of these is a defect of the motion picture as a medium, and producers of educational films are beginning to meet these objections satisfactorily. Again, limitations of costliness, of not having films and equipment available at the right time, and of acoustics, become administrative problems which are being solved as educators recognize the importance of these materials in the curriculum and adequate budgets are provided for housing, personnel, proper facilities, and materials.

A legitimate limitation is that films require projection equipment the operation of which demands skilled operators, whether they be teachers or students. And for the present at least, another limitation seems to be the need to project a film in a darkened or semi-darkened room with the companion problems of visibility and ventilation. However, attempts are now being made to solve these problems.

Materials Available in Specific Areas

A teacher should know what films, filmstrips, slides, recordings, prints, and other audio-visual materials are available for the subject, unit, or topic he is teaching or plans to teach. If there is no central audio-visual department from which to obtain these materials, he should know the nearest local source for purchase or loan. Most catalogs listing films and other aids give brief descriptions of them; a few catalogs also rate or appraise the material on the basis of its educational worth.

The following example will illustrate this point. A teacher desiring to present a unit on the development of American life in a study of American History and Problems would be concerned with teaching materials on the Colonial period, the causes and results of the Revolutionary War, the beginning of the new nation under the Articles of Confederation, the formation of the Constitution, and the domestic and foreign problems which arose as the nation grew in size and power during the early part of the nineteenth century. He would also want to use materials about some of the great men who lived in that period, such as John Adams, Samuel Adams, George Rogers Clark, Benjamin Franklin, Alexander Hamilton, Patrick Henry, Thomas Jefferson, John Paul Jones, James Madison, Thomas Paine, and George Washington. The following is a list of audio-visual materials which the teacher might compile for that particular unit and one from which he would finally choose those most suited to his pupils and most effective in achieving his teaching purposes.

Aid	Title	Source	Classification	Page
Film	*Eighteenth Century Life in Williamsburg*	EFG[3]	975.5	460
Film	*George Washington's Virginia*	SEMP[4]	171	128

[3] EFG refers to the *Educational Film Guide* (New York: H. W. Wilson Co., 1945). This reference gives the sources from which the films can be obtained.

[4] SEMP refers to *Selected Educational Motion Pictures* (Washington: American

SUGGESTED CONTENT FOR MEETING REQUIREMENTS 13

Aid	Title	Source	Classification	Page
Film	*Historic Virginia*	EFG	971.55	408
Film	*Planter of Colonial Virginia*	SEMP	325	460
Film	*Story That Couldn't Be Printed*	EFG	323.4	151
Filmstrip	*English Settlement and Colonial Conflicts*	Society for Visual Education, 100 East Ohio St., Chicago 11, Ill.		
Record	*Charter Oak* American Challenge Series (33 1/3 rpm)	Brisacher, Van Norden and Staff, Inc., Petroleum Bldg., Los Angeles, Calif.		
Record	*Declaration of Independence* Lest We Forget, Series I (33 1/3 rpm)	Institute for Democratic Education, Inc., 415 Lexington Ave., New York 17, N.Y.		
Record	*We Declare Our Independence* Lest We Forget, Series IV (33 1/3 rpm)	Institute for Democratic Education, Inc.		

The following might contribute educationally significant material to a study of the colonies' fight for independence and the new nation's struggle to form a sound national government.

Aid	Title	Source	Classification	Page
Film	*Bill of Rights*	SEMP	35	30
Film	*Boston Tea Party*	EFG	973.3	457
Film	*Boy Who Saved a Nation*	EFG	973.3	457
Film	*Declaration of Independence*	EFG	973.3	457
Film	*Declaration of Independence*	SEMP	103	77
Film	*Eve of the Revolution*	EFG	973.2	455
Film	*Flag Speaks*	EFG	929.9	433
Film	*Give Me Liberty*	EFG	973.2	456
Film	*Our Bill of Rights*	EFG	342.73	159
Film	*Our Constitution*	EFG	342.73	159
Film	*Our Declaration of Independence*	EFG	973.3	457
Film	*Our National Government*	EFG	353	160
Film	*Servant of the People*	SEMP	379	265

Council on Education, 1942). Films listed in this reference have been appraised by teachers in cooperation with the Committee on Motion Pictures in Education of the American Council on Education.

Aid	Title	Source	Classification	Page
Film	*Sons of Liberty*	EFG	973.3	457
Film	*Yorktown*	EFG	973.3	458
Record	*Articles of Confederation* Lest We Forget, Series IV (33 1/3 rpm)	Institute for Democratic Education, Inc., 415 Lexington Ave., New York 17, N.Y.		
Record	*Benedict Arnold and Major Andre* Lest We Forget, Series I (33 1/3 rpm)	Institute for Democratic Education, Inc.		
Record	*Bill of Rights* Lest We Forget, Series IV (33 1/3 rpm)	Institute for Democratic Education, Inc.		
Record	*Constitution of the United States* Cavalcade of America Series (33 1/3 and 78 rpm)	New York University Film Library, Recordings Division, Washington Square, New York, N.Y.		
Record	*The Constitution* Lest We Forget, Series I (33 1/3 rpm)	Institute for Democratic Education, Inc.		
Record	*Defending Our Constitution* Lest We Forget, Series IV (33 1/3 rpm)	Institute for Democratic Education, Inc.		
Record	*Drafting the Constitution* Teach-O-Discs (78 rpm)	Audio-Visual Division, Popular Science Publishing Co., 353 Fourth Ave., New York 10, N.Y.		
Record	*Freedom of Assembly* Lest We Forget, Series IV (33 1/3 rpm)	Institute for Democratic Education, Inc.		
Record	*Freedom of the Press* Lest We Forget, Series IV (33 1/3 rpm)	Institute for Democratic Education, Inc.		
Record	*Freedom of Religion* Lest We Forget, Series IV (33 1/3 rpm)	Institute for Democratic Education, Inc.		
Record	*Freedom of Speech* Lest We Forget, Series IV (33 1/3 rpm)	Institute for Democratic Education, Inc.		
Record	*Valley Forge* Cavalcade of America Series (33 1/3 and 78 rpm)	New York University Film Library		

SUGGESTED CONTENT FOR MEETING REQUIREMENTS 15

Aid	Title	Source	Classification	Page
Record	*The Virginia Plan* Lest We Forget, Series IV (33 1/3 rpm)	Institute for Democratic Education, Inc.		
Famous Paintings	*The Bell's First Note* *Betsy Ross* *Writing the Declaration of Independence*	Denoyer-Geppert Co., 5235 Ravenswood Ave., Chicago 40, Ill.		

The following films and records are available for that part of the unit dealing with the domestic and foreign problems that beset the new nation after the adoption of the Constitution.

Aid	Title	Source	Classification	Page
Film	*Daniel Boone*	EFG	921	428
Film	*Daniel Boone* (Feature)	Films Inc., 330 W. 42nd St., New York 18, N.Y.		
Film	*Daniel Boone*	EFG	973.2	455
Film	*Hail Columbia*	EFG	973.3	458
Film	*Kentucky Pioneers*	EFG	976.9	461
Film	*Man without a Country*	EFG		472
Film	*Monroe Doctrine*	EFG	327.73	152
Film	*Old Louisiana*	*1000 and One Bluebook*, Educational Screen, 64 E. Lake St., Chicago 1, Ill.		
Film	*Our Louisiana Purchase*	EFG	973.4	458
Film	*Our Monroe Doctrine*	EFG	327.73	152
Film	*Romance of Louisiana*	SEMP	365	255
Film	*Song of a Nation*	SEMP	397	276
Film	*Territorial Expansion of the U.S. from 1783 to 1853*	SEMP	425	294
Film	*Vincennes*	EFG	973.3	458
Filmstrip	*The Beginnings of the American Nation*	Society for Visual Education, 100 East Ohio St., Chicago 11, Ill.		
Record	*America's Second War for Independence in 1812* Lest We Forget, Series I (33 1/3 rpm)	Institute for Democratic Education, Inc., 415 Lexington Ave., New York 17, N.Y.		
Record	*Conspiracies against the New Government* Lest We Forget, Series I (33 1/3 rpm)	Institute for Democratic Education, Inc.		

Aid	Title	Source	Classification	Page
Record	*Doctor Franklin Goes to Court* Cavalcade of America Series (78 and 33 1/3 rpm)	New York University Film Library, Recordings Division, Washington Square, New York, N.Y.		
Record	Growth of Democracy Series (78 rpm)	Ideal Pictures, 2408 West 7th St., Los Angeles 5, Calif.		
Record	*Monroe Doctrine* Lest We Forget, Series IV (33 1/3 rpm)	Institute for Democratic Education, Inc.		
Record	*Star Spangled Banner* Story Behind the Song Series (33 1/3 rpm)	Training Aids, Inc., 7414 Beverly Blvd., Los Angeles 36, Calif.		

If a teacher wants to approach the study of this period through an emphasis on the leaders and their contributions or if he wishes to review the period by highlighting the lives of its great men, there are many materials to help do this job. Dramatizations of the lives of these men help to personalize history and make it real to students. The teacher can choose from these:

Aid	Title	Source	Classification	Page
Film	*Alexander Hamilton*	EFG	921	429
Film	*George Washington, His Life and Times*	SEMP	170	126
Film	*Thomas Jefferson and Monticello*	Virginia Conservation Commission, Richmond, Va.		
Filmstrip	*George Washington*	Society for Visual Education, 100 East Ohio St., Chicago 11, Ill.		
Filmstrip	*George Washington, the Father of Our Country*	Society for Visual Education		
Record	*George Rogers Clark* American Challenge Series (33 1/3 rpm)	Brisacher, Van Norden and Staff, Inc., Petroleum Bldg., Los Angeles, Calif.		
Record	*Alexander Hamilton* American Challenge Series (33 1/3 rpm)	Brisacher, Van Norden and Staff, Inc.		
Record	*Robert Morris* American Challenge Series (33 1/3 rpm)	Brisacher, Van Norden and Staff, Inc.		
Record	*Thomas Paine* Cavalcade of America Series (78 and 33 1/3 rpm)	New York University Film Library, Recordings Division, Washington Square, New York, N.Y.		

Aid	Title	Source	Classification	Page
Record	*Patrick Henry* Teach-O-Discs (78 rpm)	Popular Science Publishing Co., 353 Fourth Ave., New York 10, N.Y.		
Record	*Paul Revere* Teach-O-Discs (78 rpm)	Popular Science Publishing Co.		
Record	*Farmer, Executive, and Father of His Country— George Washington* Lest We Forget, Series II (33 1/3 rpm)	Institute for Democratic Education, Inc., 415 Lexington Ave., New York 17, N.Y.		
Record	*Father of the American Navy—John Paul Jones* Lest We Forget, Series II (33 1/3 rpm)	Institute for Democratic Education, Inc.		
Record	*Francis Scott Key* Cavalcade of America Series (78 and 33 1/3 rpm)	New York University Film Library		
Record	*Idol of the Backwoodsmen —Thomas Jefferson* Lest We Forget, Series II (33 1/3 rpm)	Institute for Democratic Education, Inc.		
Record	*John Paul Jones* American Challenge Series (33 1/3 rpm)	New York University Film Library		
Record	*The Marquis de Lafayette* American Challenge Series (33 1/3 rpm)	New York University Film Library		
Record	*Thomas Jefferson* American Challenge Series (33 1/3 rpm)	New York University Film Library		

This comprehensive, but not inclusive, listing indicates the wealth of materials available for one unit in one course. A proportionately large number of audio-visual materials are available for units in other areas of the curriculum. Teachers should compile similar lists for the units, topics, or subjects they plan to teach. Some of the larger school systems include the titles of selected audio-visual materials in their published courses of study and teachers need only to supplement them. However, for the most part, teachers will have to make up their own files of materials and their sources. Furthermore, they should preview and examine carefully as many materials as possible in order to judge their worth and to become familiar with the nature of aids they might use. How to select and use audio-visual materials for a particular teaching situation is discussed later in this section.

Sources of Materials and Equipment—Local, National, and International

The sources of audio-visual materials and equipment are as changeable as they are numerous. Old listings are seldom reliable, and current ones are generally incomplete because new companies are constantly being formed to meet the production and distribution needs of this rapidly expanding field. Because of this, teachers should be familiar both with *sources* of information about producers and manufacturers of materials and equipment and with the names of the well-established firms. They should also know the catalogs, current periodicals, and organizations in the field. The following types of information will help teachers start their own files of sources, which must be as accurate, as up to date, and as complete as possible.

1. STANDARD CATALOGS

Educational Film Guide (annual). H. W. Wilson Co., 950 University Ave., New York 52, N.Y.

Educators Guide to Free Films. Educators Progress Service, Randolph, Wis.

Films for Classroom Use. Teaching Film Custodians, Inc., 25 West 43rd St., New York 18, N.Y.

Films from Britain. British Information Services, 30 Rockefeller Plaza, New York 20, N.Y. (Branch offices in other cities.)

Index of Training Films. Eastman Kodak Co., Rochester 4, N.Y.

One Thousand and One—The Blue Book of Non-Theatrical Films. Educational Screen, 64 East Lake St., Chicago 1, Ill.

Recordings for School Use. World Book Co., Yonkers-on-Hudson, N.Y.

Selected Educational Motion Pictures. American Council on Education, 744 Jackson Place, Washington 6, D.C.

Sources of Visual Aids for Instructional Use in Schools. Pamphlet No. 80, U.S. Office of Education, Superintendent of Documents, Government Printing Office, Washington 25, D.C.

U.S. Government Films Catalog. Castle Films, 30 Rockefeller Plaza, New York 20, N.Y.

The Utilization Digest. Bell and Howell Co., 7108 McCormick Road, Chicago 45, Ill.

2. Some Sources of Educational Films

Arthur Barr Productions, 1265 Bresee Ave., Pasadena 7, Calif.
Bell and Howell Co., 7108 McCormick Road, Chicago 45, Ill.
British Information Services, 30 Rockefeller Plaza, New York 20, N.Y.
Castle Films (U.S. Office of Education Films), RCA Building, Rockefeller Center, New York 20, N.Y.
Coronet Instructional Films, Inc., 919 North Michigan Ave., Chicago 11, Ill.
Encyclopaedia Britannica Films, Inc., 20 North Wacker Drive, Chicago 6, Ill.
Films, Inc., 330 West 42nd St., New York 18, N.Y.
Frith Films, P.O. Box 565, Hollywood, Calif.
Ideal Pictures Corp., 28 East 8th St., Chicago 5, Ill.
International Film Foundation, Suite 1000, 1600 Broadway, New York 19, N.Y.
Knowledge Builders, 625 Madison Ave., New York 22, N.Y.
National Film Board of Canada, 84 East Randolph St., Chicago, Ill.
Pictorial Films, Inc., RKO Building, Radio City, New York 20, N.Y.
Teaching Films Custodians, 25 West 43rd St., New York 18, N.Y.
Vocational Guidance Co., 2718 Beaver Ave., Des Moines, Iowa
Walter O. Gutlohn, Inc., 21 West 45th St., New York 19, N.Y.
YMCA Motion Picture Bureau, 347 Madison Ave., New York 17, N.Y.

3. Lists of Producers and Distributors of Films

Some of these sources are:

Business Screen, 812 North Dearborn St., Chicago, Ill. (Current issues.)
Educational Film Guide. H. W. Wilson Co., New York 52, N.Y. (See Directory of Producers and Distributors at the end of the book.)
Educators Guide to Free Films. Educators Progress Service, Randolph, Wis. (See Source index.)
Film and Radio Guide, 172 Renner Ave., Newark, N.J. (See Audio-Visual Directory inside of back cover of current issues.)
Film World, 6060 Sunset Blvd., Hollywood 28, Calif. (See 16-mm. Film Booking Guide which appears in each issue.)
One Thousand and One—The Blue Book of Non-Theatrical Films. Educational Screen, 64 East Lake St., Chicago 1, Ill. (See Index to Producers and Distributors.)
The Audio-Visual Handbook. Ellsworth C. Dent, Society for Visual Education, Inc., Chicago, Ill. (See chapter on Sources of Information, Materials and Equipment.)

Educational Screen, 64 East Lake St., Chicago 1, Ill. (See Trade Directory for the Visual Field in each issue.)

4. FILMSTRIPS AND SLIDES

Teachers should be familiar with the main sources of filmstrips and slides, such as:

American Council on Education, 744 Jackson Place, Washington 6, D.C. (Slides and filmstrips.)
Keystone View Co., Meadville, Pa. (3¼ x 4 slides.)
Munday and Collins, 814 West 8th St., Los Angeles 14, Calif. (Slides.)
Philp Photo Service, 1218 American Ave., Long Beach 2, Calif. (2 x 2 slides.)
Popular Science Publishing Co., 353 Fourth Ave., New York 10, N.Y.
Society for Visual Education, Inc., 100 East Ohio St., Chicago 11, Ill. (Slides and filmstrips.)
The Jam Handy Organization, 2821 East Grand Blvd., Detroit 11, Mich. (Filmstrips, silent and sound.)
Three-Dimension Company, 4555 West Addison St., Chicago 41, Ill. (Slides and filmstrips.)
Visual Sciences, Box 264, East Suffern, N.Y. (Filmstrips.)

5. GOVERNMENT SOURCES

Teachers should be familiar with the most important sources of government-produced films, slides, and other pictorial materials, such as:

U.S. Department of Agriculture, Filmstrip Section, Washington, D.C.
U.S. Department of Agriculture, Office of Motion Pictures, Washington, D.C.
U.S. Department of the Interior, Washington 6, D.C.
U.S. Department of the Interior, Bureau of Mines, 4200 Forbes St., Pittsburgh, Pa.
U.S. Department of Labor, Division of Labor Standards, Washington, D.C.
U.S. Marine Corps, Constitution Ave. at 18th St., Washington, D.C.
U.S. Office of Education, Washington 25, D.C.

6. RADIO AND RECORDINGS

Teachers should know the main sources of information about radio, recordings, and transcriptions, such as:

American Broadcasting Co., 30 Rockefeller Plaza, New York 20, N.Y.
Association for Education by Radio, 228 North La Salle St., Chicago 1, Ill.
Columbia Broadcasting System, 485 Madison Ave., New York 22, N.Y.
Federal Radio Education Committee, Washington 25, D.C.
Mutual Broadcasting Co., 1440 Broadway, New York 18, N.Y.
National Association of Broadcasters, 1760 N St. NW, Washington, D.C.
National Broadcasting Co., 30 Rockefeller Plaza, New York 20, N.Y.
Popular Science Publishing Co., 353 Fourth Ave., New York 10, N.Y.
Recordings Division, New York University, Washington Square, New York 3, N.Y.
Script and Transcription Exchange, U.S. Office of Education, Washington 25, D.C.
Training Aids, Inc., 7414 Beverly Blvd., Los Angeles 36, Calif.

7. MANUFACTURERS OF EQUIPMENT

Teachers should know the names of some of the leading national manufacturers of equipment and the addresses of local dealers who handle their equipment. Most of the companies listed here have local dealers in the larger cities. This list is *not* complete.

1. Motion picture projector manufacturers, such as:

    Ampro Corp., 2835 North Western Ave., Chicago 18, Ill.
    Bell and Howell Co., 7108 McCormick Road, Chicago 45, Ill.
    DeVry Corp., 1111 Armitage Ave., Chicago 14, Ill.
    Movie-Mite Corp., 1103 East 15th St., Kansas City 6, Mo.
    Natco, Inc., 505 North Sacramento Blvd., Chicago 12, Ill.
    RCA, Victor Division, Camden, N.J.
    Victor Animatograph Corp., Davenport, Iowa

2. Filmstrip and slide projectors:

    Ampro Corp., 2835 North Western Ave., Chicago 18, Ill.
    Golde Manufacturing Co., Dept. B, 1220 West Madison St., Chicago 7, Ill.
    Society for Visual Education, Inc., 100 East Ohio St., Chicago 11, Ill.
    Three-Dimension Co., 4555 West Addison St., Chicago 41, Ill.

3. 3¼ x 4 slide projectors:

    Keystone View Co., Meadville, Pa.
    Spencer Lens Co., Buffalo, N.Y.

4. Opaque projectors:

> Spencer Lens Co., Buffalo, N.Y.
> Bausch and Lomb Optical Co., Rochester, N.Y.

5. Screens:

> Da-lite Screen Co., Inc., 2723 North Crawford Ave., Chicago 39, Ill.
> Radiant Manufacturing Co., 1144 West Superior St., Chicago 22, Ill.

6. Sound slide film and transcription players:

> The Magnavox Co., Illustravox Division, Dept. BS–5, Fort Wayne 4, Ind.
> Operadio Manufacturing Co., Dept. BV–10, St. Charles St., St. Charles, Ill.

7. Recorders:

> RCA Educational Dept., Camden, N.J.
> Recordio, Wilcox-Gay Corporation, Charlotte, Mich.

8. Maps, Prints, Posters

Teachers should know about sources of maps, study prints, three-dimension materials, and posters, such as:

A. J. Nystrom & Co., 3333 Elston Ave., Chicago, Ill. (Maps.)
Arthur Barr Productions, 1265 Bresee Ave., Pasadena, Calif. (Prints.)
Blackhurst Book Sales, Inc., 2505 Carpenter Ave., Des Moines 11, Iowa. (Charts.)
Denoyer-Geppert Co., 5235 North Ravenswood Ave., Chicago, Ill. (Maps, exhibits, etc.)
Hi Worth Pictures, 1499 East Walnut St., Pasadena 4, Calif. (Prints.)
Milton Bradley Co., New Brunswick, N.J. (Posters, exhibits, etc.)
Pictorial Statistics, Inc., 142 Lexington Ave., New York, N.Y. (Charts.)
Rand McNally & Co., 536 South Clark St., Chicago, Ill. (Maps.)
Walker & Co., 1736 Franklin St., Oakland 12, Calif. (Prints.)

9. Local Sources of Material and Equipment

Teachers should know about local sources of material and equipment, such as:

Audio-visual education departments in their own school system.
Department or division of audio-visual education in the state department of education.

SUGGESTED CONTENT FOR MEETING REQUIREMENTS 23

Local camera shops and suppliers of materials and parts.
Local equipment dealers.
Local firms which service equipment.
Local offices of the national distributors of films, filmstrips, slides, and other visual material. They should know the nearest branch office of the companies listed under section 2 (page 19).
Local producers and distributors of audio-visual materials.
Local universities which have film rental services as part of their extension divisions.

10. LOCAL COMMUNITY RESOURCES

Teachers should know about the resources in their communities which will cooperate in arranging field trips, supplying speakers, or visual and printed materials. Such lists are usually compiled as a result of surveys made by teachers.

Santa Barbara County, for instance, has published a book *Santa Barbara County Teacher's Guide for Use of Community Resources*[5] which contains listings such as the following:

1. Santa Barbara Botanic Garden
   Address: Mission Canyon Road, Santa Barbara
   Communicate with: Director
   Function: Grow, preserve, and propagate plants native to this area
   Affiliation: None
   Services available:
      Speakers: None
      Excursions: Yes
      Movies and slides: Yes
      Exhibits: None
   Printed material available: Bulletin on *Trees of California*; *Guide to Santa Barbara Botanic Garden*.
   Area or community served: Santa Barbara
2. Santa Barbara Glass Co., Inc.
   Address: 310 Chapala Street, Santa Barbara
   Communicate with: Manager
   Function: Manufacture of glass and replacement of broken glass
   Affiliation: Local distributor for Libby-Owens Co.
   Services available:
      Speakers: None

[5] *Santa Barbara County Teacher's Guide for Use of Community Resources* (Santa Barbara, Calif.: The Schauer Printing Studio, Inc., 1941).

Excursions: Yes
Movies and slides: Yes
Exhibits: Glass blocks, colored glass, etc.
Printed material available: Booklets
Area or community served: Ventura, Santa Barbara, and San Luis Obispo Counties

11. LEADING ORGANIZATIONS IN AUDIO-VISUAL EDUCATION

Teachers should know the names of leading organizations in the field of audio-visual education, such as:

Association for Education by Radio, 228 North La Salle St., Chicago 1, Ill.
Division of Visual Instruction of the National Education Association, 1201 Sixteenth St. NW, Washington 6, D.C.
Educational Film Library Assoc., 45 Rockefeller Plaza, New York 20, N.Y.
Film Council of America, 12th at Lamarr, Austin, Tex.
Educational Film Research Institute, 1133 North Highland Ave., Hollywood 38, Calif.

12. CURRENT PERIODICALS AND BULLETINS

Teachers should know current periodicals and bulletins and the areas of audio-visual education each emphasizes.

Business Screen, 812 North Dearborn St., Chicago 11, Ill.
Educational Screen, 64 East Lake St., Chicago 1, Ill.
Federal Radio Education Committee (FREC) Bulletin, U.S. Office of Education, Washington 25, D.C.
Film Forum Review, Teachers College, Columbia University, 525 West 120th St., New York 27, N.Y.
Film News, American Film Center, Inc., 45 Rockefeller Plaza, New York 20, N.Y.
Film World, 6060 Sunset Blvd., Hollywood 28, Calif.
Hollywood Quarterly, 350 Royce Hall, University of California, Los Angeles 24, Calif.
Journal of the Association for Education by Radio, 228 North La Salle St., Chicago 1, Ill.
News Letter, Bureau of Educational Research, Ohio State University, Columbus, Ohio
See and Hear, 1204 West Johnson, Madison 6, Wis.
Sight and Sound. The British Film Institute, 4 Great Russell St., London, England

Teachers will find the information outlined in the foregoing twelve sections helpful even if the school where they teach or plan to teach has an audio-visual department. Teachers should have some actual experience in using these sources. Practical problems, such as those they are likely to have on the job, should be given during their study of audio-visual education. Here is an example:

Miss Chandler is planning to teach a unit on aviation to her sixth graders as part of a social studies program which emphasizes how people have learned to transport persons and goods and the effects on our lives of this closer contact with one another. She plans to use maps, charts, films, study prints, filmstrips, recordings, and other audio-visual materials which are appropriate for sixth graders who are above average IQ. She wants to emphasize the development of transportation and its place in a modern world. She is not, at present, concerned with the technical aspects of flying or the manufacture of planes. Her school has all kinds of equipment except a silent film projector.

Problem: From the catalogs and other sources, prepare a list of materials which Miss Chandler might obtain. This list should indicate the following:

Types of material available and sources from which they may be obtained.
Which items are free.
Which items can be rented and the cost.
Which items must be purchased and the cost.
Which items may be borrowed from a local source.

Principles of Good Teaching That Affect the Selection and Use of These Materials

It is assumed that teachers in training and teachers in service will have had courses in educational psychology prior to a general consideration of educational methods and the study of audio-visual education.

Teachers should understand that the principles of good teaching are based upon a knowledge of the nature of learning and of the individual and social needs of pupils, which knowledge has been translated into effective instructional practices. Psychological principles such as the following will affect the *selection* and *use* of audio-visual teaching materials just as they should affect the selection and use of textbooks and reference materials:

1. The individuals in any class are in different stages of growth.
2. Each individual has his own rate of growth.
3. Each individual has certain basic drives.
4. Each individual has certain special interests.
5. Each individual acts as a whole and not with separate intellectual, emotional, and physical responses.
6. Learning must be purposeful.
7. Learning usually persists to the extent that it is used. A person learns what he practices.
8. Activities must be appropriate to the learning desired.
9. There is no learning without interest.
10. A close relationship exists between interest and readiness to learn.
11. There must be readiness for an experience before a pupil will be able to profit from it.
12. Interest in and enthusiasm for the thing to be learned will develop a favorable attitude toward what is being learned.
13. Difficulties in learning may be caused by many factors, some of which are outside the pupil and beyond his control. For instance, difficulties may be caused by
    a) the teacher
    b) the materials
    c) the problem under discussion
    d) the environment
    e) home conditions
    f) poor health

Selection of Audio-Visual Teaching Materials

The proper selection of audio-visual materials, based on the principles of good teaching, is an essential part of utilization and an important factor in their effectiveness as teaching tools. Selection has two phases: (1) the preliminary selection of materials for their general educational worth in terms of broad curricular objectives; and (2) the choice of specific audio-visual materials for a particular instructional situation. Preliminary selection is often made by the staffs of audio-visual departments working with teacher preview committees. Sometimes curriculum coordinators work with teachers in the selection of suitable materials. Evaluation or appraisal forms are generally used for judging the educational worth of new materials. Although

these vary widely in format and length, the criteria which are applied fall under the following headings:
1. The grade levels for which the material is suited.
2. The curriculum areas or subject fields for which it is appropriate.
3. The educational purposes or objectives which the material serves.
4. The authenticity or accuracy of the content.
5. The validity of the general impressions which the material gives.
6. The objectivity or bias of the content.
7. The effectiveness of its organization and manner of presentation for instructional purposes.
8. The technical quality.
9. The strong points and weak points of the material.

The choice of specific audio-visual materials for a particular instructional situation is made by the teacher and is based on criteria such as:
1. Is the material appropriate to the age and grade level of the pupils? The teacher must keep in mind that his pupils vary as much as three years and six months in physical age, and may vary from the third to the tenth grade in their understanding of various subjects.
2. Is it adapted to the understanding and experience of the group?
3. Is it related to the interests and needs of the pupils—needs of which they are aware?
4. Is it related to the unit being studied?
5. What will it contribute to the specific objectives of the unit or problem being studied?
6. Is it interesting?
7. Is it of suitable length? For instance, is it too long for small children whose attention span is limited?
8. Are the concepts it presents too difficult? Is the manner of presentation too complicated?
9. Is the information presented important for students to know?
10. Are the general impressions which it leaves valid in terms of other information and in terms of real-life experiences and activities?
11. What understandings should result from the use of this particular device?

12. What attitudes or appreciations are likely to result from its use?
13. What skills may be improved from its use?
14. If there is more than one type of audio-visual material available for a unit, which one or ones are most suited to my group and which will do the best teaching job in the shortest time?

Using Audio-Visual Materials

There is no "one best way" of using audio-visual materials, and the methods of use are limited only by the physical nature of the devices themselves and the skill and imagination of the teacher. Procedures basic to effective teaching with other instructional aids are likewise applicable to audio-visual materials and in general consist of four main steps:

1. Teacher preparation: selecting, planning, and preparing for the learning experience.
2. Class preparation: getting the class ready.
3. Presentation: using audio-visual materials as an integral part of the total learning situation.
4. Class follow-up: tying in what has been learned with all the related learning experiences—testing, applying, and evaluating what has been learned.

These four main steps are developed in the following outline as a general procedure for using audio-visual materials. It is to be noted, however, that good teaching practices are a necessary part of good utilization. Obviously this general pattern must be adapted to a particular classroom situation on the basis of (1) the nature of the aid itself, (2) the purposes for using it, and (3) the needs of the group.

1. Teacher preparation
   a) The teacher selects the material most suited to the needs of his group and the purposes he has for using it.
      (1) See pages 26–28 for discussion of criteria of selection.
      (2) He may have more than one purpose for using a particular teaching tool.
   b) He previews the material to be sure that it will help attain his purposes or objectives.
      (1) He notes the main points that relate to the purpose he has in mind.

(2) He thoroughly familiarizes himself with the organization of the content and its manner of presentation.

(3) In the case of films, filmstrips, slide-sets, and transcriptions he decides whether to present all of the material at a given time or only a section. He remembers that in general, learning by "wholes"—large organic units—is more efficient than by parts or small units.

c) He analyzes the nature of the learning process required for achieving the aims of the lesson and plans appropriate methods of use.

(1) If the teacher's primary aim is to develop an understanding, he must note, for instance, those parts of the film, filmstrip, record, or study print that will give a key to understanding and decide on the best methods of focusing attention on those parts.

(2) If the main purpose is to build an appreciation, then his approach and techniques must be those that lead to appreciation. For instance, questions must be designed to bring out a feeling of respect toward the spirit of determination of the writers of the Constitution, or a feeling about the value of the discovery of radium, and so on.

2. Class preparation

a) The teacher sets up the purposes of use with the students.

b) He develops a readiness for the thing to be learned by:

(1) Relating what is to be learned to the previous experiences and backgrounds of the pupils.

(2) Making sure the students understand the reason for new learning experiences.

(3) Arousing interest in the material to be used.

(a) He knows that interest is a motivating force in learning.

(b) He knows that enthusiasm and interest help to develop a favorable attitude toward the activity.

(4) Providing any additional information or background that will help students gain the most from the material to be presented.

(a) He may, for instance, explain the vocabulary which will be used, especially new words and new terms.

c) He assures active participation in the learning situation by:
  (1) Asking pupils to look for the facts, the main ideas, the general impressions, the relationships, the specific techniques, and so forth which will help achieve the purposes of the lesson.
    (*a*) He may ask different pupils to look for different things in terms of their interests and abilities.
    (*b*) He asks them to look for significant points—not trivial ones.
  (2) Anticipating the presentation with personal enthusiasm for what is to be seen or heard.
3. Presentation of the audio-visual material
  a) The teacher arranges the best possible environmental conditions for the presentation.
    (1) Audio-visual materials such as prints, posters, models, and exhibits usually do not require much change in the physical aspects of the environment.
      (*a*) For instance, if the study prints are 11 x 14 and contain important details, the teacher arranges the room so that they can be used in small informal groups or individually.
      (*b*) In the case of posters, models, and exhibits, the teacher makes provision for pupils to move about freely to view and study them.
    (2) The use of radio broadcasts, records, and transcriptions calls for an informal listening situation. The teacher arranges seating and equipment so that students may sit near the loudspeaker and in an informal grouping.
    (3) Projected audio-visual materials require special attention to room arrangements, environment, and the setting-up of equipment.
      (*a*) The teacher, with the help of students, makes provisions for:
        Room darkening, if a daylight projection box is not used.
        Adequate ventilation.
        Proper seating so that all pupils can see.

Setting up and checking equipment before use and without distracting the class.
Safeguarding the equipment.
(b) The teacher, by careful planning, makes sure physical arrangements are "relegated to unobtrusiveness."

4. Class follow-up
   a) The teacher and the students carry out appropriate follow-up activities to help further achieve the teaching purposes for which the audio-visual materials were used.
   (1) He discusses with the students the points they were to look for during the presentation of the material.
   (2) He clarifies points not understood.
   (3) He corrects errors of facts, false impressions, and so forth.
   (4) He plans with the students for oral or written reports.
   (5) He and the students plan other activities which have been stimulated by the learning experience.
   (6) He and the students plan ways of applying what has been learned either to the problem being solved, to a new project, or to a past learning experience.
   b) The teacher checks on whether the purpose has been achieved. This may be done in a number of ways.
   (1) He plans a review of what has been learned by:
      (a) Having students bring salient points together in a summary.
      (b) Having students ask each other questions.
      (c) Having students give their conclusions and the points that bear on those conclusions.
      (d) Giving review questions to bring out the relationship of facts or ideas, one to another.
      (e) Asking questions which will help students to make comparisons and generalizations.
   (2) He tests in order to measure the adequacy of what has been learned.
      (a) Tests must be appropriate to the kind of learning needed to achieve the teaching purposes. For instance, if a test is to check main ideas or general impressions, it should not be designed to measure the student's ability to remember factual details.

(b) Tests need not be complicated, nor always formal. It is sometimes possible to develop or secure other visual materials to test what has been learned *visually*. For instance, a filmstrip on the micrometer will help the shop instructor test the students on what has been gained from the film *The Micrometer*.[6]

c) The teacher and students evaluate the whole learning experience and reset their goals, if necessary. As part of this evaluation they consider the effectiveness of the methods of using a a particular device in an effort to improve the next use of the same or other audio-visual materials.

(1) The teacher may discover that attitudes which he never suspected or intended to arouse developed from the use of a certain film. This discovery may alter his decision about using the film another time or change his purpose for using it. A change of purpose will affect the methods used in the preparation period. Or he may find a filmstrip or transcription on the same subject to be more effective than the film with his particular group.

(2) The teacher remembers that, in no instance, does the mere availability of audio-visual materials determine the objectives or basic instructional content since audio-visual materials are an aid to effective instruction—not a substitute for it, or a determiner of what should be taught.

Production of Simpler Aids, Such as Mounted Prints, Handmade Slides, Filmstrips, and Photographs

Both elementary and secondary teachers should know, for instance, how to mount photographs, pictures from newspapers, magazines, and other sources. The increased use of pictures in all publications read by adults, as well as by children and youth, makes it imperative for pupils to learn to "read" pictures, to check their validity, to analyze them, and to interpret both the pictures and the accompanying captions.

Pictures should be mounted for four reasons: (1) to make them more usable; (2) to preserve them; (3) to make them more attrac-

---

[6] Castle Films (U.S. Office of Education Visual Aids Unit), RCA Building, Rockefeller Center, New York 20, N.Y.

tive; (4) to assure the psychological reaction that comes from the use of carefully prepared materials. Most audio-visual directors agree that the mounts should be uniform—possibly in two or three different sizes. Three practical sizes are: 5 x 7 mounts for pictures to be used with the opaque projector and 9 x 12 and 11 x 14 mounts for magazine pictures and similar materials.

Teachers should be able to mount pictures by the following process or by some other simple method:

Mounting Pictures by the Dry-Mount Method

1. Assemble the materials and equipment needed.
    a) Pictures to be mounted.
    b) Scissors and/or paper cutter.
    c) Pencil and ruler.
    d) Dry-mounting tissue which can be obtained in rolls and in sheets from photographic supply and stationery stores.
    e) Electric iron with heat control. Special dry-mounting irons can be obtained.
    f) Mounts. Kraft board is one of the least expensive and most satisfactory materials. Bristol board, chip board, and mat board are similar materials. Light-brown kraft board is very satisfactory if a large number of pictures are to be mounted and the teacher does not want the expense of buying a variety of materials. Other colors may be used if an artistic effect is particularly desired.
    g) Several pieces of plain white paper which are larger than the largest picture.
    h) Any clear flat lacquer and thinner. Wall-paper lacquer is good.
    i) Insect sprayer or paint sprayer—if a large number of pictures are to be preserved.
2. Mount the picture or pictures.
    a) Cut mounting board to desired size with scissors or paper cutter.
    b) Trim picture carefully.
    c) Cut dry-mounting tissue to the picture size.
    d) Measure length and width of picture and mark boundary points lightly on mount.
        (1) Top margin should be narrower than bottom margin.
        (2) Center picture between side margins.

e) Plug in electric iron and set heat control at 300° F. (approximately).

f) Place dry-mounting tissue on the back of the picture. Tack the four corners of the tissue to the back of the picture with the warm iron. Tack it in other places if the picture is large.

g) Place picture in correct position on mount.

h) Place piece of white paper over the picture and then press firmly with warm iron to make a bond. Start from center of picture and move iron slowly in a circular motion to the outside of the picture.

i) Remove the white paper and check the edges of the picture to be sure the bond has been made.

j) Mount the label or caption on the front or the back of the mount in the same manner.

k) Place books or other weights on the pictures to be sure that they do not warp or bulge.

l) Thin the lacquer according to directions on the can.

m) Spray the finished picture with the clear, flat lacquer.
   (1) If there are a large number of pictures, a paint sprayer should be used.
   (2) If only a few pictures are to be preserved, a fly sprayer can be used.

Principles and Procedures for Setting Up an Audio-Visual Education Service; How a Teacher Can Best Use This Service

If audio-visual materials are to be used effectively by teachers in the school's instructional program, *the right materials and equipment must be at the right place at the right time.* This operating principle is so basic that to disregard it or fail to provide for it may seriously hinder, if not entirely discourage, teacher use of these materials. The establishment of audio-visual education services or departments by city and county school systems is one way of making sure that the right materials and equipment are readily available to teachers when needed and of providing them with professional assistance in the methods of selection, use, and evaluation. Thus, the two major functions of a central audio-visual service become: (1) the procurement, distribution, and maintenance of teaching materials and equipment; and (2) assistance in their utilization. Each is dependent upon the other.

The individual or individuals responsible for these functions find that their duties are of two general kinds: administrative and supervisory. Administrative duties include:
1. Appointing and training assistants.
2. Selecting materials and equipping the department.
3. Determining curriculum needs.
4. Preparing a budget for the department.
5. Evaluating, selecting, and purchasing new materials, and, in some instances, equipment for schools. (In general, schools should buy their own equipment.)
6. Arranging for the distribution of materials and/or equipment.
7. Collecting and classifying materials such as study prints.
8. Providing catalogs and other information about available materials and sources.
9. Providing storage, maintenance, and repair facilities.
10. Assisting schools in solving problems of projection, darkening, storage, etc.
11. Cooperating with state offices and other departments.
12. Obtaining support for the program through public education.

Supervisory duties include:
1. Educating teachers in use of audio-visual materials and equipment.
2. Conducting faculty meetings designed to encourage better utilization.
3. Selecting and working with a committee of teachers, supervisors, and curriculum directors on problems related to the curriculum and methods of instruction.
4. Observing teacher use of audio-visual materials.
5. Planning with teachers for improved use of audio-visual materials.
6. Providing or teaching demonstration lessons.
7. Supervising local production of audio-visual materials such as slides.
8. Developing teacher guides for the materials.
9. Evaluating the instructional contributions and determining the needs of the audio-visual program.
10. Keeping teachers and others informed about new materials and important developments in audio-visual education.

A *Measure for Audio-Visual Programs in Schools* prepared by Helen Hardt Seaton for the American Council on Education discusses in Part II many of the problems of organizing visual programs. Part III (pages 31-40) contains recommendations for developing audio-visual programs in city, county, and town school systems. The planning and service functions of a department (or audio-visual education service) are described; the organization and operation of a centralized department are discussed, as well as the organization of the program within an individual school. An advisory committee of audio-visual educators (see page 2 of the publication for their names) assisted in drawing up the recommendations; hence, they represent the combined counsel of many leaders who have had actual experience as directors or supervisors of audio-visual education departments. The authors believe that these recommendations should be the basis for any consideration of principles and procedures for setting up a service.

Suggestions for the Organization of a County Audio-Visual Education Program,[7] a report prepared by a subcommittee for the Audio-Visual Aids Committee of the California School Supervisors Association, gives specific suggestions for organizing and administering a county service. A similar report on city audio-visual departments is being prepared by a subcommittee of the same association and will be published in a future issue of the *California Journal of Elementary Education*. *The School Division Film Library*[8] prepared for the Virginia State Board of Education is a practical manual of administrative procedures and discusses in detail the problems of procurement, storage, filing, distribution, maintenance, and repair.

Whether or not a school has the services of a city or county audio-visual department, the audio-visual program should be organized in each school[9] under the direction of an *audio-visual coordinator,* sometimes called a "building director." The audio-visual coordinator is usually a teacher who has been released from part or all of his other duties to take charge of securing, handling, and maintaining materials and equipment used in his school, and to assist teachers with their use. Responsibilities of the audio-visual coordinator include:[10]

[7] *California Journal of Elementary Education,* XIV (February 1946), 163–74.
[8] W. H. Durr, *The School Division Film Library* (Richmond: Bureau of Teaching Materials, State Board of Education, Commonwealth of Virginia, 1946), pp. 1–41.
[9] Helen Hardt Seaton, *A Measure for Audio-Visual Programs in Schools,* pp. 34–35.
[10] *Ibid.*

1. Informing teachers in his school about available materials.
2. Assisting teachers in the selection of materials.
3. Working with teachers in improving utilization.
4. Extending the use of audio-visual aids within the school.
5. Securing evaluation on material used.
6. Ordering audio-visual materials from the central department.
7. Scheduling aids and equipment within the building.
8. Training teachers and students in the operation of equipment.
9. Maintaining liaison between the school and the central department.
10. Supervising the collection of filmstrips, recordings, slides, flat pictures, and museum objects for the building, organizing and directing school journeys.

All of the teachers in a school or school system should be familiar with the organization and operation of their local audio-visual service or department and know how to make the most efficient use of it. If there is a school audio-visual coordinator, he should be responsible for assisting teachers and giving them information about points such as:

1. What catalogs are available and how to use them.
2. How to preview materials before making a selection.
3. Which materials have been recommended for the units of subjects they are teaching.
4. What teaching guides or manuals are available to accompany the aids.
5. How to fill out order forms or requisitions.
6. How to order equipment, if this is necessary.
7. How long different types of materials may be kept.
8. What procedures must be followed in returning materials and equipment.
9. Which staff members give technical assistance.
10. Which staff members give professional help on selecting and using materials.
11. What hours the department is open and whom to call for various types of service.

The teacher must also understand that he has a responsibility to the audio-visual department, its staff, and/or the school coordinator, in return for their material and professional assistance. He should be willing to assume responsibilities such as these:

1. Serve on preview committees for the selection of new materials.

2. Report and evaluate his use of certain aids, if requested to do so.
3. Assist in developing teacher guides for films, filmstrips, recordings, and other materials that he is using in his teaching. Pupils can sometimes help develop guides as part of their classwork.
4. Report damaged material or faulty equipment.
5. Use materials and equipment carefully.
6. Report delays or inefficiencies in the distribution of materials.
7. Return all materials on schedule.
8. Suggest improvements in services which the department can render.
9. Assemble and/or prepare materials such as slides, study prints, and exhibits which will add to the department's materials and will serve other teachers.
10. Give demonstrations of the use of materials, if requested to do so.
11. Serve on an advisory committee for the department, if requested.
12. Attend demonstrations and institutes and participate in workshops in order to learn about new materials and equipment and new methods of use.

If a teacher wants to become a school coordinator of audio-visual materials or, perhaps, looks forward to working in an audio-visual department, then he should know as much as possible about procuring, storing, filing, and maintaining the various kinds of materials and equipment, which knowledge must be gained from experience in handling them. Actual training and experience in an existing department of audio-visual education are also needed, as well as additional specialized work at the university level.

Current Trends and Practices

Teachers need to know the present status of audio-visual education in American schools and colleges, in federal, industrial, and religious training programs, and in the educational programs of other nations. They should know about the uses of these materials in the industrial, military, and incentive programs of World War II and the implications for education. Teachers should be familiar with the major research studies (pages 6–8), the sources of materials (pages 18–25), and the activities of local, national, and international organizations in this field.

General impressions similar to the following should be outcomes of the foregoing study:

1. The audio-visual approach to learning is not new.
2. Developments in audio-visual education have passed the initial stages.
3. Practically all the evidence from educational research and from military and civilian use proves beyond question the effectiveness of audio-visual materials as instructional tools.
4. Wartime training activities which used audio-visual materials capitalized on the educational research of the previous decade. Educational personnel provided leadership for many of the wartime training programs.
5. Increased use of audio-visual materials is to be found in the educational, training, and public relations programs of agencies outside the school.
6. Increased use of audio-visual materials is to be found in the educational programs of other nations.
7. The "know-how" of use is a deciding factor in the ultimate effectiveness of audio-visual materials.
8. Schools, for the most part, have been slow to apply the findings of research to educational procedures.
9. Educators should reconsider the placement of content within the curriculum and the amount of time needed to teach certain units or courses as new audio-visual materials simplify certain concepts and accelerate the learning of others.
10. Life is more complex than ever before; the individual must have more knowledge, understanding, skill, and experience to live competently in today's world. Therefore, schools have to teach more and better than ever before, and to do so, they must make *extensive and intensive* use of audio-visual materials.

Certain trends such as those given below should also be apparent from a consideration of the background and development of audio-visual education:

1. A trend toward decentralization of the centers of distribution of materials.
2. A trend toward the appointment of an audio-visual coordinator for individual schools.
3. A trend toward increased and improved teacher education in the use of audio-visual materials.
4. A trend toward the production of materials specifically planned for each area of the curriculum.

5. A trend toward increased use in adult education classes.
6. A trend toward the expanded use of *all* of the various audio-visual materials.
7. A trend toward the preparation of teachers' manuals to accompany each aid.
8. A trend toward the production of lighter equipment.
9. A trend toward the incorporation of utilization techniques into the projected and recorded aids.
10. A trend toward new research on how to produce better materials and how to use them more effectively.
11. A trend toward the selection of professional, audio-visual education personnel who are also qualified either in the field of curriculum, administration, or supervision.

III. SUGGESTIONS FOR PRE-SERVICE AND IN-SERVICE EDUCATION OF TEACHERS

PRACTICES among teacher education institutions which offer some study in audio-visual education vary widely; for the most part, they are neither systematic nor adequate. Several ways by which teacher education institutions can provide adequate training and experience in audio-visual education are suggested here. The solution of the problem does not lie in the choice of one means or another, but in attacking the problem from several of the following approaches.

Pre-Service Education of Teachers

1. Courses in audio-visual education offered by departments of education during the regular semester

    In these courses audio-visual materials should be studied in their total relationships to learning, to curricular objectives, and to methods of instruction. Although individual institutions will decide how to conduct such courses, the following considerations merit attention.

    a) The course should be taught by a qualified member of the faculty who has a broad educational background and *specialized* training and experience in audio-visual education.

    b) The content of the course cannot be presented on the purely verbal level. It must be experienced. There should be multiple opportunities for practice, for demonstration, for the use of the materials in specific situations. The instructors should actually use these materials throughout the course so that students will also learn about audio-visual materials *from* audio-visual materials.

    c) Opportunity for laboratory work is essential for two reasons:
    (1) Teachers will not use these aids unless they are thoroughly oriented in the use of the equipment and have overcome all fear of the mechanical aspects of the equipment.

(2) Precision equipment requires precision operation and care. Skill in its use is acquired *only* after considerable practice.

2. Units dealing with audio-visual education in general and special methods courses

    Such units should complement—not substitute for—the course discussed above. These units should provide further opportunities for the teacher to apply his learning to a specialized situation.

3. Units dealing with audio-visual education in courses for administrators, curriculum directors, and guidance personnel[1]

4. Use of audio-visual materials throughout the teacher education curriculum

    "The theory is that teachers are more apt to teach as they are taught than they are to teach as they are taught how to teach. In other words, if young people preparing themselves for the teaching profession are to be maximally impressed with the pedagogical and psychological importance of audio-visual curriculum materials, and if when they start teaching they are to consider audio-visual aids an integral part of the total materials available for instruction, such materials should be in actual use throughout the teacher training curriculum."[2]

5. Use of audio-visual materials in college courses outside the department or school of education

    Since most teachers have a major or minor in a special subject field, they should also have the experience of learning from the use of audio-visual materials in those areas for the same reasons as given in the preceding point.

    The development of an audio-visual materials center,[3] headed by an audio-visual education specialist, would stimulate the use of materials in all departments. The center would make materials available to all college classes and be responsible for getting equipment and materials to the right place at the right time. The specialist would be able to assist professors in the selection and use of materials.

[1] Helen Hardt Seaton, *A Measure for Audio-Visual Programs in Schools* (Washington: American Council on Education, 1944), p. 39.

[2] Stephen M. Corey, "Audio-Visual Aids and Teacher Training Institutions," *Educational Screen*, XXIV (June 1945), 226.

[3] James W. Brown and Robert B. Abbott, "An Instructional Materials Center for the Teachers College," *See and Hear*, I (November 1945), 52-59.

In-Service Education of Teachers

1. Extension courses offered in the college's service area
    a) Such courses are offered to develop competence among teachers who have had no pre-service training in audio-visual education.
    b) They serve to inform teachers about new materials and to provide further opportunities for them to acquire skill in the use of these materials.
2. An Audio-Visual Aids Center
    An Audio-Visual Aids Center or an Instructional Materials Bureau should serve the instructors, the students, and adult groups in the community.[4]
3. Summer course and workshops
    These should serve the same purposes as the extension courses, except that they should offer teachers a chance to do more intensive study and to get more practical experience through the activities of a workshop.
4. Short courses offered during the school year
    This type of course has frequently been given in agricultural education and conference leadership. The General Extension Division of the University of Florida gave a ten-day course in audio-visual education to a group of teachers who obtained leaves of absence from their school districts.[5] Short courses should consist of demonstrations, clinics, round-table discussions, previews of materials, and individual conferences on special problems.
5. Conferences, institutes, and workshops of one-, two-, or three-day duration
    These are often cosponsored by other groups such as the state department of public instruction, the state education association, a single school system, the state or regional audio-visual education association, or the radio education organization. In general, these sessions emphasize a special problem and consist of demonstrations, clinics, and discussions, and feature leaders in the field.

Example: The University of Omaha Education Improvement Institute is cosponsored by seven organizations. The Ohio State University

[4] Thurman J. White, "A University's Audio-Visual Extension Services," *Film and Radio Guide*, XIII (December 1946), 5–8.

[5] "New Approaches to Education through Materials of Instruction," (Mimeographed; Washington: American Council on Education), p. 16.

"Institute for Education by Radio" is a *national* conference which attracts educators, commercial broadcasters, and civic leaders.

6. Consultation with school staffs

    Qualified members of the faculty can give, upon request, consultant services to individual schools or school systems. Assistance would be given on

    a) Setting up continuous in-service training programs in audio-visual education for teachers.

    b) Conducting pilot programs in individual schools to establish the type of service best suited for a particular situation.

    c) Surveying the needs and making recommendations for establishing an audio-visual educational service.

    d) Evaluating existing audio-visual education services.

    e) Conducting research in schools on the value of various materials and the methods of use.

7. Preparation and publication of articles, bulletins, handbooks, monographs, and research studies

    Examples: The News Letter bulletin published by the Bureau of Educational Research of the Ohio State University, Columbus, Ohio; the *Hollywood Quarterly* magazine published by the University of California, Los Angeles; *Phonograph Records as an Aid to Learning in Rural Elementary Schools,* a handbook published by the University of New York and the State Education Department, Albany, N.Y.

IV. GUIDES FOR THE EVALUATION OF TEACHER EDUCATION PROGRAMS IN AUDIO-VISUAL EDUCATION

ACCREDITATION committees which, in some states, are responsible for evaluating the ability of universities and colleges to meet certain professional standards for the education and certification of teachers point out that they need criteria for judging audio-visual education programs. Likewise, teacher education institutions planning to provide opportunities for study and experience in this field, as well as those already offering units and courses, have indicated that they would like to know whether their present offerings or proposed programs are adequate for developing the kind of teacher competency needed. The following points from the "Report of the California Committee on Developing Standards of Teacher Competency in Audio-Visual Education"[1] are suggested as a guide for evaluating such programs and may be used as the basis of a more comprehensive evaluation form or check list.

Philosophy and general knowledge of those persons responsible for instructing teachers in the use of audio-visual teaching materials

1. Do they have an understanding of the important developments and practices in this field?
2. Do they have an understanding of the important research studies in audio-visual education?
3. Are they familiar with significant literature in audio-visual education?
4. Do they lend their support to plans and movements designed to strengthen or improve audio-visual education?
5. Do they have an understanding of the philosophical and psychological factors underlying the use of audio-visual materials?
6. Are they encouraging and directing students to do research in this field?

[1] Adapted by the authors from the "Report of the Committee on Developing Standards of Teachers Competency in Audio-Visual Education, California State Department of Education, Division of Audio-Visual Education, December 9, 1946."

Nature of the instruction and learning opportunities in audio-visual education

1. Are courses provided in this specific field?
2. Is the instruction of high quality? Have the instructors had *practical experience* in the use of audio-visual materials?
3. Does the instruction reach all students preparing to teach?
4. Are the courses academically recognized, and is adequate credit given for them?
5. Is the audio-visual approach applied in all courses where useful, thus providing instruction by example?
6. Does classroom practice reflect a knowledge and understanding of the basic principles and methods of audio-visual education and the place of these materials in the instructional program?
7. Is good audio-visual practice evidenced in the proper utilization of blackboards, display cases, bulletin boards, and other mediums of instruction adaptable to audio-visual methods?
8. Does the instruction in audio-visual education involve the study of all the important materials and actual practice with materials and equipment?
9. Have provisions been made so that students may examine and appraise materials in their teaching fields of interest?
10. Is emphasis placed on helping students to acquire skill in actually selecting and using audio-visual materials?
11. Are audio-visual materials presented in their total relationships to learning, to curriculum objectives, and to methods of instruction?
12. Are students given opportunities to demonstrate their skill in the use of audio-visual materials and equipment?

Provision of materials and equipment, and provision for the administration of the audio-visual program

1. Are audio-visual laboratory facilities provided with a wide variety of materials and equipment?
2. Are the materials and equipment sufficient to meet the needs of instructors and students, and to permit a *working* knowledge thereof?
3. Are materials and equipment up to date, properly maintained, and accessible?

4. Have personnel and facilities been provided for cataloging, storing, repairing, and maintaining materials and equipment, and for transporting them to the point of use as required?
5. Are capable and experienced personnel in charge of the program, providing it with direction, evaluating results, and planning for growth and improvement?
6. Is the library of reading materials about audio-visual materials up to date and comprehensive? Are current magazines in the field available?

Knowledge, understanding, skills, and abilities acquired by students
1. Do students utilize audio-visual materials properly in their practice teaching?
2. Do students, upon examination, give evidence of possessing adequate understanding, skills, and attitudes in the field of audio-visual education?
3. Do students satisfactorily demonstrate their skill in handling materials and equipment?
4. What do students say about their study of audio-visual education? How do they think it will help them be better teachers?

BIBLIOGRAPHY

Chapter II

PHILOSOPHICAL AND PSYCHOLOGICAL FACTORS WHICH AFFECT THE USE OF AUDIO-VISUAL MATERIALS IN THE CLASSROOM

DALE, EDGAR. *Audio-Visual Methods in Teaching.* New York: Dryden Press, 1946. Chap. i: "Visual and Auditory Methods in Teaching"; chap. ii: "Education for 'Permanent' Learning"; chap. iii: "Making Experiences Usable"; chap. iv: "The 'Cone of Experience'"; chap. v: "Moving Forward by Looking Backward."

GATES, A. I., JERSILD, A. G., McCONNELL, T. R., and CHALLMAN, R. C. *Educational Psychology.* New York: Macmillan Co., 1942. Chap. iii: "The Development of Meanings."

General Education in a Free Society: Report of the Harvard Committee on the Objectives of a General Education in a Free Society. Cambridge: Harvard University Press, 1945.

HOBAN, CHARLES F., JR. *Focus on Learning.* Washington: American Council on Education, 1942.

HOBAN, CHARLES F., HOBAN, CHARLES F., JR., and ZISMAN, SAMUEL B. *Visualizing the Curriculum.* New York: Dryden Press, 1937. Chap. i: "Why Visual Aids in Teaching."

KEPES, GYORGY. *Language of Vision.* Chicago: Paul Theobald, 1944. Pp. 6-50.

McKOWN, HARRY C., and ROBERTS, ALVIN B. *Audio-Visual Aids to Instruction.* New York: McGraw-Hill Book Co., 1940. Chap. ii: "The Functions of Audio-Visual Aids in Learning."

MUNRO, PAUL. *Encyclopaedia of Educational Research.* New York: Macmillan Co., 1941. "Philosophy of Education," pp. 798-801.

MURSELL, JAMES L. *Education for American Democracy.* New York: W. W. Norton & Co., 1943. Chap. iii: "American Education Finds a Policy"; chap. x: "The Problem of Teaching."

Newer Instructional Practices of Promise. 12th Yearbook, Department of Supervisors and Directors of Instruction. Washington: National Education Association, 1939.

New Methods vs. *Old in American Education: Report on Evaluation of Newer Practices in Education.* New York: Bureau of Publications, Teachers College, Columbia University, 1941. Pp. 1-14, 52-54.

PRESCOTT, DANIEL A. *Emotion and the Educative Process.* Washington: American Council on Education, 1938. Chap. ii: "Basic Affective Phenomena"; chap. iv: "Patterning and Trainability of Affective Behavior"; chap. vii: "The Influence of Affective Factors upon Learning"; chap. ix: "Affect and Education."

PRESSEY, S. L., and ROBINSON, F. P. *Psychology and the New Education.* New York: Harper & Bros., 1944.

RENSHAW, SAMUEL. *Psychological Optics.* Duncan, Okla.: Optometric Extension Program, 1939. Chap. v: "Seeing as a Habit"; chap. vi: "Seeing as Visual Perception"; chap. x: "Some Further Characteristics of Visual Perception."

WRINKLE, W. L., and GILCHREST, R. S. *Secondary Education for American Democracy.* New York: Farrar & Rinehart, 1942.

RESEARCH STUDIES AND THEIR IMPLICATIONS FOR INSTRUCTION

ARNSPIGER, V. C. *Measuring the Effectiveness of Sound Pictures as Teaching Aids.* Teachers College Contributions to Education, No. 565. New York: Columbia University Press, 1933.

ATYEO, H. C. *The Excursion as a Teaching Technique.* New York: Bureau of Publications, Teachers College, Columbia University, 1939.

BELL, REGINALD, CAIN, LEO F., LAMOREAUX, LILLIAN A., et al. *Motion Pictures in the Modern Curriculum: A Report on the Use of Films in the Santa Barbara Schools.* Washington: American Council on Education, 1941.

CHARTERS, W. W. *Motion Pictures and Youth.* New York: Macmillan Co., 1933.

CONSITT, FRANCES. *The Value of Films in History Teaching.* London: G. Bell & Sons, Ltd., 1931.

DALE, C., DUNN, F. W., HOBAN, CHARLES F., JR., and SCHNEIDER, ETTA. *Motion Pictures in Education: A Summary.* New York: H. W. Wilson Co., 1938. See Part V of this book for a summary of some of the more important researches.

EICHEL, CHARLES G. "An Experiment to Determine the Most Effective Method of Teaching Current History," *Journal of Experimental Education,* IX (September 1940), 37–40.

FIELD, HARRY, and LAZARSFELD, PAUL F. *The People Look at Radio.* Chapel Hill: University of North Carolina Press, 1946.

FREEMAN, F. N., et al. *Visual Education.* Chicago: University of Chicago Press, 1924.

HANSEN, J. E. "The Effect of Educational Motion Pictures upon the Retention of Informational Learning," *Journal of Experimental Education,* II (September 1933), 1–4.

HOBAN. *Focus on Learning.*

KNOWLTON, D. C., and TILTON, J. W. *Motion Pictures in History Teaching*. New Haven: Yale University Press, 1929.

MELTON, A. W., and FELDMAN, F. G. *Experimental Studies of the Education of Children in a Museum of Science*. New Series, No. 15. Washington: American Association of Museums, 1936.

NATIONAL INDUSTRIAL CONFERENCE BOARD. *Visual Aids in Industrial Training*. New York: National Industrial Conference Board, 247 Park Ave., 1943.

RAMSEY, GRACE F. *Educational Work in Museums of the United States*. New York: H. W. Wilson Co., 1938.

ROULON, P. J. *The Sound Motion Picture in Science Teaching*. Harvard Studies in Education, Vol. XX. Cambridge: Harvard University Press, 1933.

TOWER HILL SCHOOL, WILMINGTON, DELAWARE (STAFF OF). *A School Uses Motion Pictures*. Washington: American Council on Education, 1940.

VANDER MEER, ABRAM W. "Economy of Time in Industrial Training," *Journal of Educational Psychology*, XXXVI (February 1945), 65–90.

WEBER, J. J. *Comparative Effectiveness of Some Visual Aids in Seventh Grade Instruction*. Chicago: Educational Screen, Inc., 1922.

WISE, H. A. *Motion Pictures as an Aid in Teaching American History*. New Haven: Yale University Press, 1939.

WITTICH, W. A., and FOWLKES, J. G. *Audio-Visual Paths to Learning*. New York: Harper & Bros., 1946.

WOELFEL, NORMAN, and TYLER, I. KEITH. *Radio and the School*. New York: World Book Co., 1945.

WOOD, B. D., and FREEMAN, F. N. *Motion Pictures in the Classroom*. Boston: Houghton Mifflin Co., 1929.

CHARACTERISTICS OF THE COMMON TYPES OF AUDIO-VISUAL MATERIALS

DALE. *Audio-Visual Methods in Teaching*. Part II: "Audio-Visual Teaching Materials."

DENT, ELLSWORTH C. *The Audio-Visual Handbook*. Chicago: Society for Visual Education, 1946. Chap. ii: "Types of Visual Aids and Their Uses"; chap. iii: "Types of Sound Aids for Schools"; chap. iv: "Types of Audio-Visual Aids to Instruction."

DECHERT, CURT. *A New Approach to the Use of Modern Instructional Materials*. Chicago: The Educational Screen, 1945.

FREEMAN. *Visual Education*.

HOBAN. *Focus on Learning*. Pp. 9, 15, 24, 67, 94–96.

HOBAN, HOBAN, and ZISMAN. *Visualizing the Curriculum.* Chap. ii: "The School Journey"; chap. iii: "Objects and Models—The School Museum"; chap. iv: "The Motion Picture"; chap. v: "Arresting Life with the Camera—The Still Picture"; chap. vi: "Graphic Materials." For specific references to motion pictures, see pp. 96, 101–6, 113, 114, and 118–20.

McKOWN and ROBERTS. *Audio-Visual Aids to Instruction.* Chap. iv: "Objects, Specimens, and Models"; chap. v: "Graphic Materials"; chap. vi: "Flat or Unprojected Pictures"; chap. vii: "Projected Still Pictures"; chap. viii: "The Motion Picture"; chap. ix: "School Trips and Tours"; chap. x: "Auditory Aids."

"New Approaches to Education through Materials of Instruction." Mimeographed. Washington: American Council on Education, 1937.

REEVES, C. E. *Standards for High School Teaching.* New York: D. Appleton & Co., 1932. Pp. 279-81.

U.S. NAVY DEPARTMENT. BUREAU OF NAVAL PERSONNEL. *More Learning in Less Time.* NavPers 1300. Washington: Bureau of Naval Personnel, 1943. Pp. 6.

WITTICH and FOWLKES. *Audio-Visual Paths to Learning.* Pp. 11, 15, 16, 18–20.

SELECTION AND USE OF AUDIO-VISUAL TEACHING MATERIALS

BARR, A. S., BURTON, W. H., and BREUCKNER, LEO J. *Supervision.* New York: D. Appleton-Century Co., 1938. Pp. 261–66.

BOSSING, NELSON L. *Progressive Methods of Teaching in Secondary Schools.* Boston: Houghton Mifflin Co., 1935.

BRIGGS, THOMAS H. *Improving Instruction: Supervision by Principals of Secondary Schools.* New York: Macmillan Co., 1938. Chap. xi: "Purposes for Teachers"; chap. xii: "Purposes for Pupils."

DALE. *Audio-Visual Methods in Teaching.*

DENT. *The Audio-Visual Handbook.* Chap. iv: "Types of Audio-Visual Aids to Instruction."

GILES, H. H. *Teacher-Pupil Planning.* New York: Harper & Bros., 1941. Chap. iii: "On the Nature of Human Needs"; chap. iv: "On the Nature of Learning."

GREENE, HARRY A., JORGENSEN, ALBERT N., and GERBERICH, J. RAYMOND. *Measurement and Evaluation in the Secondary Schools.* New York: Longmans, Green & Co., 1943.

Group Planning in Education. 1945 Yearbook, Department of Supervision and Curriculum Development. Washington: National Education Association, 1945.

HOBAN. *Focus on Learning.*
HOBAN, HOBAN, and ZISMAN. *Visualizing the Curriculum.* Pp. 129–34.
KARCH, R. RANDOLPH, and ESTABROOKE, EDWARD C. *250 Teaching Techniques.* Milwaukee: Bruce Publishing Co., 1943.
LEE, J. MURRAY, and LEE, DORIS MAY. *The Child and His Curriculum.* New York: D. Appleton-Century Co., 1940. Chap. ii: "The Child as a Growing Organism"; chap. iii: "The Child as a Developing Personality"; chap. iv: "The Child as Motivated by Purposes and Interests"; chap. v: "The Child as a Learner"; chap. viii: "Materials and Experiences."
LEONARD, P., and EURICH, A. C. *An Evaluation of Modern Education.* New York: D. Appleton-Century Co., 1942.
The Measurement of Understanding. 45th Yearbook, Part I, National Society for the Study of Education. Chicago: University of Chicago Press, 1946.
MONROE, WALTER S. (Ed.). *Encyclopaedia of Educational Research.* New York: Macmillan Co., 1941. "Evaluation," pp. 468–70.
Multi-Sensory Aids in the Teaching of Mathematics. 18th Yearbook, National Council of Teachers of Mathematics. New York: Bureau of Publications, Teachers College, Columbia University, 1945.
MURSELL. *Education for American Democracy.*
MURSELL, JAMES L. *The Psychology of Secondary School Teaching.* New York: W. W. Norton & Co., 1939.
Newer Instructional Practices of Promise. 12th Yearbook, Department of Supervisors and Directors of Instruction. Washington: National Education Association, 1939.
NOEL, FRANCIS W. *Projecting Motion Pictures in the Classroom.* Washington: American Council on Education, 1940.
PRESSEY and ROBINSON. *Psychology and the New Education.*
ROBERTS, H. D., RACHFORD, H., and GOUDY, E. *Airlanes to English.* New York: McGraw-Hill Book Co., 1942.
The Training of Secondary School Teachers: Especially with Reference to English. Report of a Joint Committee of the Faculty of Harvard College and of the Graduate School of Education. Cambridge: Harvard University Press, 1942.
WRINKLE and GILCHRIST. *Secondary Education for American Democracy.*

Magazine references on uses of audio-visual teaching materials

AHL, FRANCES NORENE. "The Use of Audio-Visual Aids in an International Relations Class," *Educational Screen*, XXIV (March 1945), 102–4, and 110.

BARTS, NORMA A. "Techniques of Using Films in Classroom Teaching," *Educational Screen*, XXV (May 1946), 270–71.
BERGH, BEATRICE. "On Wings We Go," *See and Hear*, I (May 1946), 59–64.
BRANDWEIN, PAUL F. "A Film in the Lesson," *See and Hear*, I (January 1946), 77–83.
COREY, STEPHEN M. "The Importance of Perceptual Learning," *Educational Screen*, XXV (November 1945), 394-97, and 404.
CRILLY, BERTHA L. "The Documentary Enters the English Classroom," *See and Hear*, I (September 1945), 21–26.
DELANEY, C. "The Film and International Understanding," *Educational Screen*, XXIV (January 1945), 17–19.
DIXON, DOROTHY I. "Community Resources Pave the Way," *Educational Screen*, XXII (February 1943), 47–51.
DURR, W. H. "Promoting Better Film Utilization," *See and Hear*, I (December 1945), 31–33.
ELDRIGE, DONALD A., and BRANDON, LEONIE M. "Utilizing the Potential Power of the Reading and Study Film," *See and Hear*, I (January 1946), 65–69.
EMBRY, H. W. "The Motion Picture in Remedial Reading," *See and Hear*, I (October 1945), 72–81.
FOWLKES, JOHN GUY. "Selecting Globes, Maps and Charts," *See and Hear*, I (October 1945), 64–66.
GERNETZKY, CARL. "Through the Looking Glass," *See and Hear*, I (December 1945), 26–30.
GORTON, RAYMOND F. "Why I Use Films in the Teaching of Biology," *Educational Screen*, XXIV (January 1945), 15–16.
GUILFORD, MARTHA. "With the Masters: Developing Art Appreciation through Visual Aids," *Educational Screen*, XXIV (January 1945), 20–22.
HAMBURG, JOHN. "The Teacher Evaluates Films," *See and Hear*, I (September 1945), 41–45.
HAMILTON, JOHN L. "Film + Teacher + Motivation = Learning," *Educational Screen*, XXIV (May 1945), 183–84.
HANKAMMER, O. A. "Camera Hunt-Project for Every Classroom," *See and Hear*, I (September 1945), 46–52.
HARTLEY, WILLIAM H. "Living Our History," *See and Hear*, I (December 1945), 85–93.
HARTLEY, WILLIAM H., and CARY, WILLIAM H., JR. "Toward Understanding Our Allies," *See and Hear*, I (December 1945), 72–81.
HERRICK, VIRGIL E. "Measure for Measure," *See and Hear*, I (May 1946), 25–30.

Johnson, Donovan, "Toward Living Mathematics," *See and Hear*, I (May 1946), 19-24.

McCarty, H. B. "Creative Art by Radio," *See and Hear*, I (May 1946), 55-59.

Meienburg, Claire. "Before the Word—The Idea," *See and Hear*, I (September 1945), 41-45.

Miller, Josephine S. "Releasing Creative Imaginations," *See and Hear*, I (October 1945), 16-20.

Millman, Ellen. "New Horizons for Primary Tots," *See and Hear*, I (October 1945), 10-15.

Olsen, Edward G. "Perspective of Audio-Visual Education," *Educational Screen*, XXV (March 1946), 120-22.

Russell, David H. "Evaluation of the Elementary School Program," *California Journal of Elementary Education*, XIII (February 1945), 183-92.

Sanders, Daisy Daily. "Seeing Our Neighbors," *See and Hear*, I (May 1946), 54-58.

Sheppard, Mildred. "Fun with Maps and Globes," *Educational Screen*, XXV (May 1946), 236-38.

Stilley, Laura. "The Use of Visual Aids in the First Grade," *Educational Screen*, XXII (January 1942), 9-11.

Tyler, Ralph W. "The Place of Evaluation in Modern Education," *Elementary School Journal*, XLI (September 1940), 19-27.

Williams, Velda M. "Down the Three Lane Highway," *See and Hear*, I (December 1945), 34-45.

Williamson, E. G. "Youth Looks to the Future," *See and Hear*, I (December 1945), 66-71.

Wrightstone, J. W. "Techniques for Measuring Newer Values in Education," *Journal of Educational Research*, XXXV (March 1942), 517-24.

Audio-visual materials

Film Tactics. 16-mm. sound film; running time, 20 minutes. Source: Castle Films, Inc., Rockefeller Center, New York 20, N.Y.

Tips on Slide Films. Silent filmstrip. Source: Jam Handy Organization, 2821 East Grand Blvd., Detroit 11, Mich.

Learning to Live. 16-mm. sound film; running time, 20 minutes. Source: British Information Services, 30 Rockefeller Plaza, New York 20, N.Y.

Using the Classroom Film. 16-mm. sound film; running time, 20 minutes. Source: Encyclopaedia Britannica Films, Inc., 20 North Wacker Drive, Chicago 6, Ill.

Production of Simpler Aids

ALEXANDER, MARIE E. "Preparing and Filing Mounted Materials," *Aids to Teaching in the Elementary School*. Thirteenth Yearbook, Department of Elementary School Principals. Washington: National Education Association, 1934. Pp. 194–98.

AUGHINBAUGH, B. P. "So You Want to Make Lantern Slides," *Film and Radio Guide*, XIII (December 1946), 10–12.

"Bibliography of References on Making of Slides," *See and Hear*, II (November 1946), 31.

BONWELL, WILLIAM A. "Effective Slides Made by Teacher and Pupil," *Aids to Teaching in the Elementary School*. Thirteenth Yearbook, Department of Elementary School Principals. Washington: National Education Association, 1934. Pp. 319–29.

BROOKS, MARY ESTHER. "Lantern Slides and How to Make Them." *See and Hear*, I (April 1946), 65–71. Also November 1946, pp. 29–30.

COLLINS, EARLE S. "Training Prospective Teachers in Making and Using Visual Aids," *Educational Screen*, XXV (June 1946), 301–2.

DENT. *The Audio-Visual Handbook*. Pp. 45–46, 56–65.

GALE, ANN. "The Air Age: In Handmade Lantern Slides," *Educational Screen*, XXII (March 1943), 101.

———. "The Atomic Bomb: In Handmade Lantern Slides," *Educational Screen*, XXIV (November 1945), 409.

———. "Buy Good Design: In Handmade Lantern Slides," *Educational Screen*, XXIV (June 1945), 241.

———. "Recognition of Trees: In Handmade Lantern Slides," *Educational Screen*, XXIV (February 1945), 75.

———. "Safety with Fire: In Handmade Lantern Slides," *Educational Screen*, XXV (March 1946), 128.

HAAS, KENNETH B., and PACKER, HARRY Q. *The Preparation and Use of Visual Aids*. New York: Prentice-Hall, Inc., 1946. Pp. 42–45, 110–12.

HAMILTON, G. E. "How to Make Handmade Lantern Slides," Meadville, Pa.: Keystone View Co., 1946.

HOBAN, HOBAN, and ZISMAN. *Visualizing the Curriculum*. Pp. 194–98.

LOS ANGELES CITY SCHOOLS, AUDIO VISUAL EDUCATION SECTION, OFFICE OF THE ILLUSTRATOR. *Directions for Making Handmade Lantern Slides*. Los Angeles: City Schools.

McKOWN and ROBERTS. *Audio-Visual Aids to Instruction*. Pp. 109–10, 135–38.

NELSON, ELMER R. "Lilliputia," *See and Hear*, I (May 1946), 87–94.

NEWKIRK, LOUIS V. *Construction of Lantern Slides and Maps*. Chicago: Board of Education, 228 North La Salle St., 1936.

PARK, JOE. "Butterflies: How to Collect, Rear and Preserve Them," *See and Hear*, I (April 1946), 82–87.
STERNIG, JOHN. "Homemade Visual Aids," *See and Hear*, I (April 1946), 82–87.
STUDEBAKER, JOHN W. "Terrain Models for Every School," *See and Hear*, I (February 1946), 49–55.
U.S. OFFICE OF EDUCATION. *School Use of Visual Aids*. Bulletin 1938, No. 4. Washington: Superintendent of Documents, 1938. Pp. 44–45.
VAN HORN, MARY. "We Make Our Own Instructional Material for Reading," *Educational Screen*, XXIV (June 1945), 233–34.
WEIMER, B. R. "Model Making," *See and Hear*, I (April 1946), 90–93.
WINSEY, A. REID. "Art and the Small Color Slide," *Educational Screen*, XXIV (November 1945), 398–402, and 407.

PRINCIPLES AND PROCEDURES FOR SETTING UP AN AUDIO-VISUAL EDUCATION SERVICE; HOW A TEACHER CAN BEST USE THIS SERVICE

BLACKWELL, DOROTHY. "Post-War Planning for the Audio-Visual Program in St. Louis," *Educational Screen*, XXIII (October 1944), 344–46.
BRUNSTETTER, M. B. "Housing an Audio-Visual Materials Center," *Nation's Schools*, XXXIV (December 1944), 34–35.
DALE. *Audio-Visual Methods in Teaching*. "Administration of Audio-Visual Materials," pp. 407–87.
DENT. *The Audio-Visual Handbook*. Chap. v: "Organizing the Audio-Visual Service"; also pp. 46–48, 74–75, 79–80.
DURR, W. H. *The School Division Film Library*. Richmond: Bureau of Teaching Materials, State Board of Education, Commonwealth of Virginia, 1946.
FRYE, LESLIE E. "Financing a Program of Audio-Visual Aids," Committee Report, *See and Hear*, I (January 1946), 30–34.
GREGORY, WILLIAM M. "Portable Observation Cases for Specimens and Products," *See and Hear*, I (October 1945), 59–63.
GUNN, HENRY M. "A Superintendent Looks Ahead," *See and Hear*, II (November 1946), 26–27.
HAMILTON, RUTH A. "Bringing the Library into the Curriculum," *See and Hear*, I (September 1945), 75–79.
HOBAN, HOBAN, and ZISMAN. *Visualizing the Curriculum*. Chap. viii: "Administering a Visual Aids Program"; also pp. 78–81, 155, 165–66, 193–94.

How to Run a Film Library. Chicago: Encyclopaedia Britannica Films, Inc., 1945.
JOHNSON, WALTER. "Film and Slide Booking," *Educational Screen,* XXII (March 1943), 89–90.
McKOWN and ROBERTS. *Audio-Visual Aids to Instruction.* Chap. xiv: "Administration and Supervision of the Audio-Visual Program"; also pp. 113–15, 133–34, 139–40, 167–68, 172–73.
MOYANO, SYLVIA M. "We Put Movies to Work," *Educational Screen,* XXIV (March 1945), 100–1.
NIXON, ROBERT B. "Getting Our Front Yard in Order," *Educational Screen,* XXV (March 1946), 125–26.
OWEN, HENRY J. "First Experiences with the Visual Education Program," *See and Hear,* I (January 1946), 17–22.
PATTINGTON, M. G. "Visual Education in the Smaller Central School," *Educational Screen,* XXIV (November 1945), 403–4.
SEATON, HELEN HARDT. *A Measure for Audio-Visual Programs in Schools.* Washington: American Council on Education, 1944.
"Suggestions for the Organization of a County Audio-Visual Education Program." A report prepared by a subcommittee for the Audio-Visual Aids Committee of the California School Supervisors Association, *California Journal of Elementary Education,* XIV (February 1946), 163–74. A digest of this report appeared in *See and Hear,* I (February 1946), 77–84. Also reprinted by the Division of Audio-Visual Education, California State Department of Education, Sacramento, Calif.
TIPPETT, JAMES S. *Schools for a Growing Democracy.* Boston: Ginn & Co., 1936. Chap. vi: "A Materials Bureau."
WHITE, MARIAN K. "Building from the Ground Up," *Educational Screen,* XXV (March 1946), 125–26.

CURRENT TRENDS AND PRACTICES

ANDREWS, H. L. "The Use of Audio-Visual Aids in an Airlines Training School," *Educational Screen,* XXIII (November 1944), 388–90.
Audio-Visual Education Bulletin. Washington: Educational Research Service, Research Division, National Education Association, February 1946.
Business Screen. A Report on the Training Film Program of the United States Navy, entire issue No. 5, VI (June 1945), 18–120; and A Report on Activities of Army Pictorial Service, Signal Corps, entire issue No. 1, VII (January 1946), 15–97. Chicago: Business Screen Magazine, Inc.

California Journal of Secondary Education. What the Army and Navy Are Teaching Us about Visual Aids, a symposium, XIX (January 1944), 15-39.

CRAKES, C. R. "Straws in the Wind," *See and Hear,* I (December 1945), 60-61.

CHAMBERS, M. M. *Opinions on Gains for American Education from Wartime Armed Services Training: A Preliminary Exploratory Report.* Washington: American Council on Education, 1946. Pp. 14, 21.

DALE. *Audio-Visual Methods in Teaching.* "The Future of Audio-Visual Materials"; also pp. 521-30.

DAMERON, VERNON D. "N.E.A. and Audio-Visual Education," *See and Hear,* I (January 1946), 50-52.

DENT. *The Audio-Visual Handbook.* Chap. i: "The Status of Audio-Visual Instruction."

FLYNT, RALPH C. M. "Use of Training Aids by Army and Navy," *Higher Education,* II (September 1945), 1-3.

FREEMAN, FRANK N. "Visual Education from a Twenty-five Year Perspective," *Educational Screen,* XXV (January 1946), 15-16.

GREENE, WESLEY. "The Wartime Use of Films in Canada," *Educational Screen,* XXII (March 1943), 86-88, and 93.

HART, GARDNER L. "Unexplored Areas of Visual Education," *Educational Screen,* XXV (June 1946), 300.

HOBAN, CHARLES F., JR. "What the Schools Can Learn from the Army's Film," *Educational Outlook,* XIX (March 1945), 1-10.

"Industry Increasingly Turns to Films as Business Aid," *Film World,* III (January 1947), 21.

KINDER, JAMES S. "Motion Pictures and Adult Education," *Educational Screen,* XXIV (February 1945), 56-57, and 62.

LINS, L. JOSEPH. "Survey of Audio-Visual Aids Used in Wisconsin Schools," *See and Hear,* I (September 1945), 53-58.

McNABB, J. H. "Training Millions-with-Movies," *Educational Screen,* XXII (March 1943), 97-98.

MCKOWN and ROBERTS. *Audio-Visual Aids to Instruction.* Chap. i: "The Scope of Audio-Visual Instruction."

MILES, JOHN R., and SPAIN, CHARLES R. *Audio-Visual Aids in the Armed Services: Implications for American Education.* Washington: American Council on Education, 1947.

NATIONAL INDUSTRIAL CONFERENCE BOARD. *Visual Aids in Industrial Training.*

New Horizons for Business Films: A Report of the A.N.A. Film Study. New York: Association of National Advertisers, Inc., 1946.

NOEL, FRANCIS W. *The Navy Turns to Training Aids.* Camden, N.J.: The Education Department, RCA Victor Division, Radio Corporation of America, 1944. Reprint of three articles which appeared in the *School Executive* in February, March, and April, 1944.

NOEL, F. W., and NOEL, E. G. "Looking Ahead Twenty-five Years in Audio-Visual Education," *Educational Screen*, XXV (February 1946), 67–69.

RAKESTRAW, BOYD B. "Objectives of Department of Visual Instruction, N.E.A." *See and Hear*, I (September 1945), 59–61.

ROBERTS, ALVIN B. "Scanning the Nation's Visual Education Programs: A Graph Story," *See and Hear*, I (October 1945), 30–39.

Training in the Armed Forces with Special Attention to Implications for Postwar Education in New York City. Report of a Special Committee appointed by the Superintendent of Schools. New York: Board of Education of the City of New York. Pp. 16–19, 69–70.

U.S. Office of Education. *Use of Training Aids in the Armed Services.* Bulletin 1945, No. 9, Washington: Government Printing Office, 1945.

WENDT, PAUL. "Viewing the New in Audio-Visual Education," *See and Hear*, I (September 1945), 81–86.

WITTICH and FOWLKES. *Audio-Visual Paths to Learning.* Chap. i: "The Development of the Motion Picture."

Chapter III

BROWN, JAMES W., and ABBOTT, ROBERT B. "An Instructional Materials Center for the Teachers College," *See and Hear*, I (November 1945), 52–59.

"College Radio Conference at Stephens," *Journal of the Association for Education by Radio*, VI (December 1946), 62–63.

COREY, STEPHEN M. "Audio-Visual Aids and Teacher Training Institutions," *Educational Screen*, XXIV (June 1945), 226–27.

CYPHER, IRENE L., and RAMSAY, GRACE F. "A Museum Inaugurates a 'Visual Aids Institute,' " *Educational Screen*, XXIV (February 1945), 60–62.

DE BERNARDIS, AMO. "In-service Training for Better Audio-Visual Utilization," *See and Hear*, I (April 1946), 44.

FEDERAL RADIO EDUCATION COMMITTEE WITH THE CO-OPERATION OF THE U.S. OFFICE OF EDUCATION. *Suggested Courses in Radio Broadcasting.* Washington: Federal Radio Education Committee and U.S. Office of Education, 1945.

FLECK, HENRIETTA. "Teacher Training and Audio-Visual Materials," *See and Hear*, I (May 1946), 80–86.

GNAEDINGER, W. G. "Audio-Visual Services of the State College of Washington," *Film and Radio Guide,* XIII (December 1946), 53.

HAMILTON, RUTH A. "Visual Education Demonstration for Omaha Teachers," *Educational Screen,* XXIV (March 1945), 105-7.

HANSON, G. L., and MILLER, JANE. "Teacher Training for Tomorrow," *See and Hear,* I (April 1946), 29-32.

HARDY, BROOKS. "Time to Spare," *See and Hear,* I (September 1945), 27-31.

LONG, WATT A. "Evaluation of Radio Institutes," *Journal of the Association for Education by Radio,* VI (December 1946), 58.

MURSELL. *Education for American Democracy.* Chap. xiv: "The Role and Responsibilities of the Teacher."

ROWLAND, W. T., and THOMAS, R. LEE. "Learning to Live," *See and Hear,* I (May 1946), 50-53.

SEATON. *A Measure for Audio-Visual Programs in Schools.*

WHITE, THURMAN J. "A University's Audio-Visual Extension Service," *Film and Radio Guide,* XIII (December 1946), 5-8.

WORTHY, HALEY D. "Arizona Schools Make Use of Audio-Visual Techniques," *Educational Screen,* XXV (January 1946), 21.

American Council on Education Studies

Publications of the American Council on Education are issued in the form of books, pamphlets, and *The Educational Record*, a quarterly journal.

The AMERICAN COUNCIL ON EDUCATION STUDIES, established by the Executive Committee of the Council in February 1937, are issued from time to time to present reports of divisions and committees of the Council and special studies by staff members.

SERIES I. REPORTS OF COMMITTEES AND CONFERENCES

1. *The Testing Movement.* 39 pp. 1937. Out of print
2. *Government and Educational Organization.* 44 pp. April 1937. 25¢
3. *The Student Personnel Point of View.* 14 pp. 1937. Out of print
4. *Major Issues in Teacher Education.* 44 pp. February 1938. 40¢
5. *Cooperation and Coordination in Higher Education.* 110 pp. April 1938. 50¢
6. *Fellowships in Education: A Proposal.* 15 pp. November 1938. 10¢
7. *Business Education at the College Level.* 30 pp. March 1939. 25¢
8. *School Buildings and Equipment.* 30 pp. 1939. Out of print
9. *Coordination of Accrediting Activities.* 46 pp. October 1939. 40¢
10. *Educational Research: Its Nature, Essential Conditions, and Controlling Concepts.* By Henry W. Holmes, et al. 186 pp. November 1939. $1.00
11. *Educational Studies and Their Use.* 74 pp. January 1940. 40¢
12. *Deliberative Committee Reports in Secondary Education.* 37 pp. September 1940. 25¢
13. *Organizing Higher Education for National Defense.* Edited by Francis J. Brown. 67 pp. March 1941. 50¢
14. *Cooperation in Accrediting Procedures.* 56 pp. April 1941. 50¢
15. *Higher Education Cooperates in National Defense.* 34 pp. November 1941. 25¢
16. *Higher Education and the War.* 184 pp. February 1942. $1.00
17. *Nursing Education for National Service.* 35 pp. May 1942. 25¢
18. *A Design for General Education.* Edited by T. R. McConnell. 186 pp. June 1944. $1.25
19. *Channeling Research into Education.* 187 pp. 1944. Out of print
20. *New Directions for Measurement and Guidance.* By Ralph W. Tyler, et al. 103 pp. August 1944. 80¢
21. *Motion Pictures for Postwar Education.* By Mark A. May. 23 pp. October 1944. 20¢
22. *Religion and Public Education.* 76 pp. February 1945. 75¢
23. *United States Activities in International Cultural Relations.* By I. L. Kandel. 102 pp. September 1945. 75¢
24. *Emergency Problems in Higher Education.* Edited by Francis J. Brown. 120 pp. August 1946. $1.00
25. *Use of Audio-Visual Materials toward International Understanding.* Edited by Helen Seaton Preston. 168 pp. November 1946. $1.25
26. *The Relation of Religion to Public Education: The Basic Principles.* By the Committee on Religion and Education. 54 pp. April 1947. $1.00
27. *Selected Issues in Education: Universal Military Training; Federal Aid to Education; Federal Department of Health, Education, and Security; The United Nations Educational, Scientific and Cultural Organization.* Edited by Francis J. Brown. 17 pp. April 1947. 30¢
28. *National Projects in Educational Measurement: Report of 1946 Invitational Conference on Testing Problems.* Edited by K. W. Vaughn. June 1947.

SERIES II. MOTION PICTURES IN EDUCATION

1. *The Motion Picture in Education: Its Status and Its Needs.* 24 pp. 1937. Out of print
2. *Teaching with Motion Pictures: A Handbook of Administrative Practice.* By Dale and Ramseyer. 59 pp. 1937. Out of print
3. *A School Uses Motion Pictures.* By the Staff of Tower Hill School. 118 pp. September 1940. $1.00
4. *Films on War and American Policy.* By Blake Cochran. 63 pp. 1940. Out of print
5. *Projecting Motion Pictures in the Classroom.* By Francis W. Noel. 53 pp. December 1940. 50¢
6. *Motion Pictures in a Modern Curriculum: A Report on the Use of Films in the Santa Barbara Schools.* By Reginald Bell, et al. 179 pp. May 1941. $1.00
7. *Students Make Motion Pictures: A Report on Film Production in the Denver Schools.* By Brooker and Herrington. 142 pp. May 1941. $1.00
8. *A Measure for Audio-Visual Programs in Schools.* By Helen Hardt Seaton. 40 pp. October 1944. 40¢
9. *Foundations for Teacher Education in Audio-Visual Instruction.* By Elizabeth Goudy Noel and J. Paul Leonard. 60 pp. July 1947. 75¢

SERIES III. FINANCIAL ADVISORY SERVICE

1. *College Finance.* By Lloyd Morey. 16 pp. November 1935. 10¢
2. *Depreciation of Real Property in Educational Institutions.* 9 pp. 1935. Out of print
3. *The Balance Sheet in College and University Financial Reports.* 10 pp. 1936. Out of print
4. *Current Investment Practices of Colleges and Universities.* By George E. Van Dyke. 23 pp. May 1936. 10¢
5. *Current Practices of Colleges and Universities in Obtaining Professional Counsel and Services.* 8 pp. 1936. Out of print
6. *Fitting the Accounting System to the Plan of Reporting Recommended by the National Committee on Standard Reports.* By Lloyd Morey. 13 pp. April 1936. 10¢
7. *Training for College and University Business Administration.* 12 pp. April 1937. 10¢
8. *Endowment Income and Investments, 1926-35.* By A. Robert Seass. 21 pp. April 1937. 10¢
9. *Principles of College and University Business Practice.* 7 pp. July 1937. 10¢
10. *Reporting Current Income and Expenditures.* By A. Robert Seass. 21 pp. August 1937. 10¢
11. *Statements of Fund Transactions in Financial Reports.* By A. Robert Seass. 18 pp. November 1937. 10¢
12. *Independent Audits of Colleges and Universities.* 13 pp. 1938. Out of print
13. *College and University Business Organization.* 26 pp. 1938. Out of print
14. *Endowment Income and Investments, 1926-1937.* 16 pp. 1938. Out of print
15. *Funds Subject to Annuity Agreements.* By J. Harvey Cain. 33 pp. April 1939. 25¢
16. *Inventory of Plant Assets.* By Clarence P. Slater and J. Harvey Cain. 37 pp. 1939. Out of print
17. *Auditing of Colleges and Universities.* By J. Harvey Cain. 74 pp. March 1940. 50¢
18. *Endowment Investments and Income, 1926-1939.* 28 pp. 1940. Out of print
19. *What Is Happening to College and University Investments and Income?* By J. Harvey Cain. 41 pp. June 1941. 35¢

20. *College and University Investments and Income, 1925-41.* 29 pp. July 1942. 40¢
21. *College Investments under War Conditions.* By J. Harvey Cain. 39 pp. September 1944. 40¢

SERIES IV. AMERICAN YOUTH COMMISSION

1. *Surveys of Youth: Finding the Facts.* By D. L. Harley. 106 pp. 1937. Out of print
2. *How to Make a Community Youth Survey.* By M. M. Chambers and Howard M. Bell. 45 pp. January 1939. 25¢

SERIES V. COUNCIL STAFF REPORTS

1. *Living and Learning.* By C. R. Mann. 90 pp. September 1938. 50¢
2. *Psychological Examinations, 1939 Norms.* By L. L. Thurstone, Thelma Gwinn Thurstone, and Dorothy C. Adkins. 56 pp. May 1940. 25¢
3. *Psychological Examinations, 1940 Norms.* By Thurstone and Thurstone. 41 pp. May 1941. 10¢
4. *Psychological Examinations, 1941 Norms.* By Thurstone and Thurstone. 42 pp. May 1942. 10¢
5. *Acceleration in the Colleges.* By C. S. Marsh. 29 pp. February 1943. 25¢
6. *Psychological Examination for College Freshmen, 1942 Norms.* By Thurstone and Thurstone. 32 pp. May 1943. 10¢
7. *Higher Education, Philanthropy, and Federal Tax Exemptions.* By J. Harold Goldthorpe. 40 pp. May 1944. 50¢
8. *Psychological Examination for College Freshmen, 1943 Norms.* By Thurstone and Thurstone. 28 pp. June 1944. 10¢
9. *Psychological Examination for College Freshmen, 1944 Norms.* By Thurstone and Thurstone. 29 pp. June 1945. 10¢
10. *Psychological Examination for College Freshmen, 1945 Norms.* By Thurstone and Thurstone. 34 pp. May 1946. 10¢
11. *Psychological Examination for College Freshmen, 1946 Norms.* By Thurstone and Thurstone. 23 pp. June 1947. 25¢

SERIES VI. PERSONNEL WORK IN COLLEGES AND UNIVERSITIES

1. *Educational Counseling of College Students.* By Bragdon, Brumbaugh, Pillard, Williamson. 61 pp. April 1939. 50¢
2. *Occupational Orientation of College Students.* By Cowley, et al. 74 pp. April 1939. 50¢
3. *Social Competence and College Students.* By Esther Lloyd-Jones. 89 pp. September 1940. 50¢
4. *Religious Counseling of College Students.* By Thornton W. Merriam, *et al.* 77 pp. April 1943. 50¢
5. *Counseling and Postwar Educational Opportunities.* 13 pp. May 1944. 10¢
6. *Student Personnel Work in the Postwar College.* By Willard W. Blaesser, *et al.* 95 pp. April 1945. 75¢
7. *Financial Assistance for College Students.* By Russell T. Sharpe, *et al.* 113 pp. September 1946. $1.00
8. *Counseling for Mental Health.* By Kate Hevner Mueller, *et al.* August 1947.

SERIES VII. SCHOOL PLANT RESEARCH

1. *Specification for Folding Chairs.* 39 pp. February 1942. 35¢
2. *Specification for Chair Desks.* 30 pp. March 1942. 25¢
3. *The Utilization of School Sanitary Facilities.* 35 pp. June 1942. 10¢

www.ingramcontent.com/pod-product-compliance
Lightning Source LLC
Chambersburg PA
CBHW070939240426
43667CB00036B/2437